T0243235

THE
VIKING
CODE

THE
VIKING
CODE

THE ART AND SCIENCE
OF NORWEGIAN
SUCCESS

ANDERS INDSET

WILEY

Library of Congress Cataloging-in-Publication Data

Names: Indset, Anders, author.
Title: The Viking code : the art and science of Norwegian success / Anders
    Indset.
Description: Hoboken, New Jersey : John Wiley & Sons, 2025. | Includes
    bibliographical references and index.
Identifiers: LCCN 2024024612 (print) | LCCN 2024024613 (ebook) | ISBN
    9781394288762 (hardback) | ISBN 9781394288786 (adobe pdf) | ISBN
    9781394288779 (epub)
Subjects: LCSH: Success—Norway. | Performance—Norway. | Values—Norway. |
    Norway—Civilization.
Classification: LCC BF637.S8 I535 2025 (print) | LCC BF637.S8 (ebook) |
    DDC 158.109481—dc23/eng/20240624
LC record available at https://lccn.loc.gov/2024024612
LC ebook record available at https://lccn.loc.gov/2024024613

COVER DESIGN: PAUL MCCARTHY
AUTHOR PHOTO: © ALEX KRAUS
VIKING HELMET: © GETTY IMAGES | ENDLESS STUDIO

SKY10081044_080524

Contents

Preface: You're Allowed to Defy the Law of Jante

~~The Law of Jante~~

~~You're not to think you are anything special.~~
~~You're not to think you are as good as we are.~~
~~You're not to think you are smarter than~~
~~we are.~~
~~You're not to imagine yourself better than~~
~~we are.~~
~~You're not to think you know more than we do.~~
~~You're not to think you are more important~~
~~than we are.~~
~~You're not to think you are good at anything.~~
~~You're not to laugh at us.~~
~~You're not to think anyone cares about you.~~
~~You're not to think you can teach us anything.~~

In the heart of Norway, protected, near the Swedish border, lies the small but culturally rich town of Røros. With its charming wooden houses and old copper mines, Røros has proudly raised the "UNESCO World Heritage" shield and made a name for itself far beyond its national borders. The mountain town has retained its authentic charm and historical significance, and I am a proud "Rørosing."

Through solidarity and cohesion in their closely knit community, built on an open and trustful culture, one might almost call the village of Røros "Typisk Norsk"—typically Norwegian.

It was in Røros where I grew up.

Here in the highlands, I was glued to the TV on January 1, 1992, when then-Prime Minister Gro Harlem Brundtland, with a strong voice, told the whole country in the New Year's address: "The [soccer] girls, the handball girls, the skiing boys, and the Oslo Philharmonic Orchestra: they are at the top of the world. We also want to prove that the Norwegian economy can compete internationally. Do we perhaps need a new motto? Typically to be Norwegian means to be good."

While other regions and countries are famous for certain things, it is not so easy to find something that can be described as typically Norwegian. Yes, there is brown cheese (Brunost), and Norwegians spend their Easter days at the cabin with the chocolate "Kvikk Lunsj" and their backpacks—but these are just (superfluous) objects. Are there any defining Norwegian values?

As a patriot, I have followed Norway's sporting successes all my life. I have cheered for my fellow countrymen and still watch them on TV today, even though I emigrated 23 years ago. Every 4 years, the Winternation sweeps the medals at the Olympics. But with the advantageous initial conditions—that there is snow at all—it would be presumptuous to label a high-performance culture as "typically Norwegian." Or is there a hidden secret here?

The interest in "peak performance" was an integral part of my childhood. It wasn't that I had one vision of becoming the world's best; I was more interested in progress. I had "micro-ambitions":

getting a little better every day, participating in every training session, doing something every day myself.

I still remember a time in my life, which now seems almost absurd, when I managed to complete at least one training session for 716 consecutive days—meticulously documented in my training diary. I was obsessed with learning, with making progress, with getting better.

And yet, there's something about the concept of performance (or "high-performance") that is slightly challenging. High performance can indeed be fascinating, but it can also trigger stress responses and have negative impacts.

For me, performance should be viewed positively, worthy of being highlighted. This book shines a spotlight on performance. It takes its cue from the achievements of athletes who have tapped into this greater potential, and I seek to explore what feats might be achievable through our inherent potential. To substantiate this scientifically, modern research also comes into play.

The vision of being the best in the world is not reprehensible. Striving for perfection can be a powerful motivator. The reality, however, is that we can't all build rockets to take humanity to space, we can't all create software companies that change the world, we can't all win Nobel Prizes, and we can't all stand atop the podium as world champions or Olympic gold medalists in highly competitive sports. It's more about finding the basis for progress tailored to our own standards.

This book is about discovering an inner drive that leads to positive outcomes for ourselves and enables a powerful life, regardless of whether we receive applause. It's about exploring the unlimited potential of each individual—one's own possibilities and capabilities, not just performance itself. At its core, every human being has the potential to change the current culture of how we look at success.

It's about finding the positivity in "performance," understanding the power of progress, encouraging others, and unleashing one's own potential. It's the quest for the driving force that leads to success and the essence of a positive performance culture that is creative and moves away from ego-boosting and the pursuit of money and medals at any cost.

The Viking Code shows how we can all lead more meaningful lives by rejoicing in our own successes while simultaneously cheering on others to create a conscious culture of learning and progress.

In this book, we dive into the narrative of a modern Viking culture that is not anchored in the past but firmly looks toward the future. It's not about barbaric conquests or daring historical comparisons. Instead, a story unfolds that leads us into a world yet unknown—our future. It's the vision of a positive future based on progress. In business, politics, education, and society, we discover a new compass to guide us: the Viking Code.

Rosenborg, Røros, and Radio Moments

Back before the real birth of the Internet, it was the radio and, of course, TV, where we could draw inspiration from our role models. I spent countless Sundays on the lawn in front of our house listening to my favorite soccer team, Rosenborg from Trondheim, on the radio. The "Go'Fot Theory" (the theory of the preferred foot, which was about playing the other players well) of manager Nils Arne Eggen still shapes a special culture today, immortalized with a statue of the gesticulating and screaming coach in front of the stadium. The highlight was undoubtedly the 2-1 victory in 1996 against AC Milan at the San Siro stadium and the associated advance to the quarterfinals of the Champions League.

I was also glued to the box in 1998. A whole nation cheered for legendary coach "Drillo" with his rubber boots, "Kick-and-Run" strategy, and his "Farmers from the North"—the Norwegian national team—as they knocked Brazil out of the Soccer World Cup. The handball and soccer women, well, they have always been good, and yes, being good at skiing is indeed typical in Norway.

But I wasn't just a spectator. My childhood in Røros was marked by playing all kinds of sports and a will to improve every day. Preparing for a typical Wednesday could include looking for long underwear and a thick hat, cleaning the rifle for the biathlon, filling the sports bag with resin and short pants for the later handball session, and clearing the snow from in front of the garage in order to get to my cross-country skiing, biathlon, and handball lessons. These daily sports activities created a purposeful life in mass and high-performance sports.

Even today, I let myself get carried away and fascinated by typical tasks on regular days. I still firmly believe that activity and sports are an essential part of my career and have led to successes in other areas and that you can learn a lot from playing sports for life.

The Law of Jante: A Pillar of Nordic Humility and Collective Consciousness

My childhood was also shaped by my mother's attitude, rooted in the Scandinavian "Law of Jante," which can be summed up as follows:

"You shall not believe you are anything."

Published by the Norwegian-Danish author Aksel Sandemose in his novel *A Fugitive Crosses His Tracks*, this unwritten social code of conduct traces its origins to the early twentieth century, but its implications resonate far beyond its historical confines.

Sandemose, drawing from his own experiences in the town of Nykøbing Mors in Denmark, immortalized a set of 10 principles that underscore a pervasive sentiment: the community comes before the individual, and one should never believe they are better or more important than anyone else. Though it might seem constraining on the surface, the Law of Jante is a collection of humility, egalitarianism, and unity. It not only influences personal behaviors and relationships but has also carved pathways in the sociopolitical landscapes of Nordic countries.

The Law of Jante

You're not to think you are anything special.
You're not to think you are as good as we are.
You're not to think you are smarter than
we are.
You're not to imagine yourself better than
we are.
You're not to think you know more than we do.

You're not to think you are more important
than we are.
You're not to think you are good at anything.
You're not to laugh at us.
You're not to think anyone cares about you.
You're not to think you can teach us anything.

The Law of Jante mirrors the Ten Commandments of Moses and forms a sarcastic escalation with the same message rooted in each commandment. It serves as a critique of social constraints. The historical heritage of the Law of Jante is profound. Its echoes are found in the egalitarian policies of the Nordic welfare states, the value placed on collaborative successes, and the deep sense of fraternity.

In particular, during my childhood in the 1980s and 1990s, and with my generation, it was primarily a finger-pointing at all those who positioned themselves above their social groups, or at all those who thought they were "better" than anyone else. It was similar to other cultures like Japan, where they proverbially say "A nail that sticks out gets hammered down" or to Australia and New Zealand with their "Tall Poppy Syndrome."

The "Tall Poppy Syndrome" describes the sociocultural phenomenon in which individuals who stand out due to their exceptional performances, abilities, or successes are often criticized, avoided, or downplayed, much like the tallest poppy in a field is cut down to preserve equality. It is a reflection of our human tendency to seek equality and yet often dampen the glow of excellence, which is ultimately also the intention of the Law of Jante.

I now see the Law of Jante through two lenses. On the one hand, it laid the foundation for values intrinsic to a Norwegian culture that's admired globally. Understanding Jante reveals the core of the Scandinavian identity: a society that uplifts the collective, values humility, and nurtures a distinct balance of individual freedom tethered to communal responsibility. On the other hand, this cultural tenet seems to have capped individual self-confidence and self-worth. Such qualities are not only essential in today's competitive and multifaceted society, but they might also shape the very bedrock of trust and relationships in a profoundly different manner.

For athletes, the very nature of their profession demands them to stand out, to strive for personal bests, and to break records. It necessitates a belief in oneself that often transcends what's considered ordinary. So, how does one reconcile a culture that frowns upon standing out with the intrinsic desire to excel and be the best in their field?

To overcome this syndrome, it takes courage and determination to grow and bloom despite headwinds—to stand upright, even if one stands out higher than the rest.

Needless to say, the cultural principle of the Law of Jante has strongly shaped Norway. For me, it was certainly part of the obstacle to being able to enjoy personal successes and progress. Looking back, it created a conflict between my own performance drive and talent and a recurring insecurity and lack of self-confidence, namely, that one is never good enough. So, I grew up with the ambivalent struggle between selfish ambition, which was seen as positive according to the American principle, and the suppression of individuality and personal development.

Versatility, Cohesion, and Community Spirit

My mother always emphasized values and did everything to impart this to her children. She was supportive and only wanted the best for us. What she probably meant by teaching us the Law of Jante was that one can indeed believe in oneself, that one is something, but one should not show it to others. In other words, don't boast about your accomplishments and leave your feet on the ground.

In Røros, we created an environment where activity, fun, and community work formed a unique performance culture. We won trophies and celebrated successes in team sports such as soccer and handball and individually in winter disciplines. With only 3,500 inhabitants, this small community produced numerous successful athletes from my age group alone. Hans became a biathlete, Krister was among the best cross-country skiers in Norway, Christian played soccer, Erik is a gifted musician, and Kristoffer and Håvard had professional careers as handball players in the German Bundesliga. The good "environment" and our diversity contributed our top performance to our social group.

At that time, I was hardly aware that this path was any different than the "American dream" we saw on TV. Our coaches also applied a different leadership style than those I got to know later on my journey through Europe, and that I have since come to know through my work—from authoritarian training and leadership styles in Eastern Europe to Baltic ball wizards with a unique formula for success that has produced remarkable soccer, basketball, and handball players over decades.

However, this book is not about my path, and the Viking Code is not a historical narrative. Rather, it's a deep dive into the present.

"Over night" a new generation of Norwegian athletes has conquered the world stage and is currently attracting global attention in almost all major sports. Their "surprising" successes create the feeling of something new, unprecedented. They are praised and valued, are team players, and practice fair play. Examples include Erling Haaland and Martin Ødegaard, two of the world's greatest soccer players; Viktor Hovland and Caspar Ruud, respectively, among the best golf and tennis players in the world; Karsten Warholm, who reinvented the 400-meter hurdles; the two best triathletes in the world; and even the two best beach volleyball player in the world.

The Swedish newspaper *Aftonbladet* published a view of the performance of the Norwegians in very different sports: "What's up with this country?" The Austrian *Der Standard* ventured an attempt:

> The Norwegians are outdoor people. Even caregivers of the smallest children are obliged to bring their charges into nature every day—regardless of the weather. The discussion about the daily gym lesson would be incomprehensible to anyone in Norway.

In a world dominated by many tales of rapid success and sudden genius, I find myself pondering: What is the secret behind Norway's triumph? What lessons could the global economy, educational systems, and political decision-makers learn from this unique Norwegian culture that embodies both peak performance and fundamental values? Is it possible that what I call the Viking Code can shed light on the dark corners of our most pressing global dilemmas?

A new culture of achievement has been born in Norway. Today, we find self-assured modern Vikings with a solid foundation of values everywhere.

Is this typically Norwegian? Does the Law of Jante no longer apply? Can the Viking Code teach us something on a global scale? Can we collectively mobilize a new culture of performance, one that is rooted in values? Can this new performance culture help us address current challenges in business, politics, education, and society?

These questions led me to a man whose name—Marcel Da Cruz—might sound more at home in the alleys of Rio de Janeiro than on the snow-covered slopes of Oslo. Despite his exotic name and equally impressive personality, athletic trainer Marcel is in many ways the living embodiment of the Viking Code. Together with him, we delve deeply into the essence of the code in the first part of this book. It's time to introduce you to Marcel.

PART

I

Unearthing Hidden Talents

"It's like a coltsfoot growing through concrete."

Marcel pauses to ensure I've grasped the essence of his analogy. He is a sucker for details. I have just learned about the subtle differences between choosing a "cortado" and the challenges of making a good cappuccino.

With Marcel, his perfectionism is palpable.

He has an innate ability to find beauty in intricacies, lending an ethereal quality to his words and demeanor. As I listen, I can't help but be pulled into his orbit, drawn to his every word. There's a resonance, an alignment of thought and spirit, as we delve deeper into the world of intrinsic motivation and the thirst for progress.

Marcel and I find ourselves nestled in Kaffestuggu, an age-old coffee haunt situated on one of the two primary streets in Røros. This quaint village bears witness to centuries of history, with artwork and architecture echoing its almost 400-year evolution as a mining town. Capturing the essence of what makes Røros uniquely captivating is a challenge. Yet, its "success," mirroring life and achievement, was inspired by experts from Erzgebirge in Germany to the visionary "consultants" from Trondheim. The myriad influences, hues, creators, and inspirations amalgamate into a delightful "Smörgåsbord" of distinction.

Remarkably, this is only the second time Marcel and I are meeting face-to-face, following a fleeting encounter at a local tavern a few years ago. Marcel's spouse hails from Røros, which serendipitously allowed our schedules to align, granting us this shared moment in Røros to reflect upon the developmental strides of recent decades. The familiarity between us belies the brevity of our acquaintance. Our exchanges flow effortlessly, reminiscent of a genial tennis match, where the objective is mutual exploration and understanding of the other's skills and core competencies.

Marcel unites theory and practical experience. In his days as a basketball shooting guard, Marcel bore witness to diverse training cultures and emerging talents spanning the globe.

Marcel and I establish a common ground, mutually enriching our perspectives and venturing beyond Norwegian borders in search of the elusive formula for success. We're both drawn to the enigma we've termed the Viking Code. Specifically, we're intrigued by the genesis of high-performance cultures.

Our conversation drifts to the former Soviet Union's strategy—carving regions into specialized hubs. Lithuania, for instance, emerged as the epicenter for nurturing basketball prodigies. Whenever a promising talent—much like the resilient coltsfoot—surfaced in other Soviet territories, they were promptly relocated to Lithuania's rigorous training camps. This strategy bore fruit, evident in the prominence of Lithuanian athletes in the NBA, an impressive feat for a nation of merely three million.

Or take the city of Split in Croatia, for instance. Comparable in size to Norway, Croatia has a special tradition for world-class athletes, and the city of Split seems to attract talent magnetically, molding them into stars in tennis, basketball, and soccer. Marcel's interactions with Marin Čilić shed light on the region's unique capacity to consistently produce overachievers. This reminds me of the pioneering work of Rasmus Ankersen, who, in his book *The Gold Mine Effect*, looks into the making of such global high-performance hotspots. Tragically, Ankersen's own promising soccer career was cut short by a severe knee injury during his professional debut at age 21. This setback led him to transition into a "talent anthropologist," authoring other notable works like *Winner's DNA* and *Hunger in Paradise*. Today, he wears multiple hats: director of soccer at Southampton, president of Göztepe, and a part-time chairman of the Danish Superliga club, FC Midtjylland.

But high-performance endeavors are not just engineered and built; they often have a significant element of serendipity, or what one might call "happening by chance." Humans, by nature, tend to seek explanations, sometimes even when there aren't any. We're prone to retrospectively charting our paths, creating a clear, linear narrative leading to our crowning achievements.

The Viking Code is not a mere "one-size-fits-all" blueprint. Instead, it digs deep, elucidating the intricacies and multifaceted components of cultivating high performance. When we infuse "values" into this equation, the intricacy, unsurprisingly, intensifies. It isn't a singular hotspot or sponge absorbing talent. It's more analogous to fungi, naturally dispersed over Norway's expansive 1,700 kilometer stretch. There isn't a mystical formula, a dedicated region, or even a specific sport that encapsulates Norwegian success. That's the allure for us. Our explorations suggest this success could be the outcome of cultural evolutions uniquely positioning Norway to foster numerous athletes. Interestingly, this historical pattern might not even resonate with the present-day youth.

High performance is intricate, with many intertwined components. Yet, one fundamental truth emerges: *success mandates sheer will.*

In this part of the book, we show how you can secure an early advantage—becoming uncatchable—in order to lay a solid foundation for the path to greatness.

What about talent? Well, talent is everywhere. Or as Steven Levitt and Stephen Dubner, in their 2005 bestseller *Freakonomics*, argue, "This whole idea of raw talent and genius is vastly overrated." They argue that "if you look at anybody in the world who's really, really good at anything, the odds are that they were not so great at that when they were a little kid." Marcel cites Norwegian soccer player Martin Ødegaard as an example. Martin's coach emphasized how practice, specialized training, and the right guidance honed Martin's skills from a young age. This begs the question: why did only Martin flourish and not his peers? Didn't they undergo similar training? Ultimately, the pursuit of success and high performance is a personal choice. Undeniably there are instances of exceptional talent, but there is more to it.

Marcel's metaphor of the coltsfoot exemplifies resilience, urging us to recognize the boundless potential inherent in the human spirit. Just as the coltsfoot sprouts from unlikely places, so do many great achievers, underscoring that talent is ubiquitous and success attainable for all, a phenomenon that we will also take a closer look at in this part of the book.

Our shared quest is to decipher the Norwegian success story beyond just high performance.

What's the secret ingredient that has propelled Norwegian athletes to unparalleled achievements? How do societal values factor in?

We'll take a closer look at the tradition of "dugnad," examine Norway's triumph over the limiting Law of Jante, and highlight the significance of joy, fun, and what we term "micro-ambitions."

Perhaps even more intriguingly, we'll ponder whether this success was meticulously orchestrated and engineered.

Was this global domination a result of deliberate strategies, resources, and structure?

Or did a substantial portion emerge per chance?

Through this exploration, we will uncover counterintuitive success factors and hope to uncover lessons for our ongoing human journey of pushing boundaries and achieving greatness.

First, let's take a closer look at the mystical Law of Jante.

1

Overcoming the Law of Jante: Trust Thyself

Du skal ikke tro at du *er* noe.
Du skal ikke tro at du *er* noe.
Du skal ikke tro at du *er* noe.

MENTION TO ANY Norwegian the phrase, "You should not think that you are something," and they'll instantly recognize it as a reference to the Law of Jante code of conduct.

Overcoming the Law of Jante was at the forefront of my mind when I first contacted Marcel to chat over coffee recently. It was one of the first things I mentioned to him, seeking insights to decipher the Viking Code that I had been pondering.

"Working on a book project," I texted via WhatsApp, "I need just five minutes of your time. Are you available? When would be a good time for you?"

Marcel's response came within minutes: "How about tomorrow night, around 5 p.m. to 6 p.m.?"

Our conversation kicked off with light chit-chat. As it turns out, Marcel had been working with a former roommate and teammate from my handball days in Germany. Having established our "connection," I got straight to the point.

"I'm writing a book on the Norwegian high-performance culture. It's intriguing how so many Norwegian athletes have been rising to the top across so many disciplines. The working title is *The Viking Code*, and I'd really value your insights on it."

I could feel Marcel's excitement through the phone. "That sounds amazing. I'd love to contribute. This is something I've pondered over the years myself."

I went on, "Beyond their athletic success, I've observed a distinct self-confidence and new strength of character in these athletes. They're not just elite performers but are also recognized as team players, embodying values of fairness and kindness in their sport. I think this story is both timely and unique. Could it be that Norway has overcome the Law of Jante?"

Marcel paused. "That's an interesting angle," he continued.

After another reflective moment, he added, "Count me in. This project sounds fascinating."

I couldn't help but feel a swell of joy. I had just engaged one of the world's top athletic trainers, who, for me, embodied the ideal blend of deep-rooted Norwegian understanding, combined with a cutting-edge knowledge of contemporary science and high-performance training.

Suddenly, Marcel interjected, "I believe Tutta played a significant role in overcoming the Law of Jante."

His remark transported me back to garden parties south of Oslo, overlooking the Fjord in the late 1990s. Back then, I was enrolled at NTG (Norges Toppidrettsgymnas), a high school established in 1981 initially as an alpine-focused institution. Today, it spans seven cities, offering programs in 14 different sports disciplines. NTG's hallmark is its comprehensive and tailored approach, harmonizing academics with rigorous training and fostering tight-knit relationships between students and their dedicated mentors. In essence, NTG stands as a premier academy for budding athletes, ensuring they don't compromise their education.

Numerous sports legends are alumni of this esteemed school, including biathlon maestro Ole Einar Bjørndalen, NHL star Mats Zuccarello Aasen, Olympic cycling champion Thor Hushovd, and alpine sensation Lasse Kjus, to name just a few.

I was part of the handball division in Bærum, a suburb of Oslo. My classmates excelled in various disciplines: soccer players, tennis players, cyclists, motocross drivers, chess prodigies, rowers, basketball players, runners, swimmers, and, notably, golfers. One emerging sports sensation at the time was the renowned "Tutta."

The Female Tiger Woods

Suzann "Tutta" Petersen, often dubbed the "Female Tiger Woods" on the Women's PGA Tour, emerged from Norway to secure 15 LPGA Tour victories and 7 Ladies European Tour wins. Who would have imagined that Norway would produce one of the world's premier female golfers?

At my school's garden parties, while we attempted to drive balls into the valley, aiming for the Fjord, Tutta consistently outshone everyone. Neither my sturdy bandy and hockey classmates, inspired by Adam Sandler's 1996 character in *Happy Gilmore*, nor the top-tier golfers in our class could match her drives. Beyond her evident skill, Petersen exuded a unique confidence. By age 12, Petersen told her dad she aimed to become the world's best golfer. By 14, she had meticulously outlined in a binder her vision for a professional golf career.

Looking back, there was something distinct about Petersen. While she seemed to gain greater recognition internationally than domestically, she had a uniqueness not typically seen in

Norwegian athletes. In 2015, the *New York Times* published an article titled "Suzann Pettersen's Competitiveness Is Not Seen as the Virtue It Is for Men." This piece referenced a controversial moment at the Solheim Cup in Germany that year when Petersen was involved in a dispute over an unconceded 18-inch par putt on a decisive hole. Many of her competitors believed the controversy was unwarranted.

In her unfiltered documentary, *Her Final Putt: Suzann Pettersen's Story*, she reflects on her highs and lows, detailing her relentless journey to the top. While Petersen had her rough edges, she undeniably challenged the Law of Jante and traditional Norwegian values. She was akin to a coltsfoot breaking through the pavement.

The Mozart of Chess

Marcel and I picked up on another pivotal moment. A few years after Petersen's breakthrough, a 13-year-old boy squared off against the legendary chess player Garry Kasparov. Viewers watched as Kasparov, then nearing the end of his illustrious career, arrived late to face the boy who would soon earn the moniker "The Mozart of Chess." The young prodigy, Magnus Carlsen, was also a product of Norway's NTG system, like Petersen. That day, he achieved a draw against Kasparov—a feat that marked the dawn of an unparalleled chess career. At the time of writing, Carlsen boasts a plethora of titles and has been the undisputed number-one ranked chess player since 2011.

Carlsen's influence extends beyond the chessboard. He has kicked off soccer matches at the iconic Santiago Bernabéu Stadium for his beloved Real Madrid. In 2010, he shared the spotlight with actress Liv Tyler in a G-Star ad campaign, with his likeness adorning massive billboards throughout New York. Under the guidance of his father—who has worn the hats of coach, sparring partner, and manager—Carlsen has elevated chess to a spectacle, drawing unparalleled attention to the game. With the highest chess rating in history, Carlsen hasn't merely led global rankings for more than a decade; he's exemplified to Norwegians that with the right combination of skill, dedication, and mindset, anyone—even from a small nation like Norway—can ascend to unparalleled heights.

Both Pettersen and Carlsen seem to have instigated a cultural shift in Norway, challenging the traditional constraints of the Law of Jante.

Yet another iconic Norwegian figure followed high achievers, sparking my initial thoughts on Norwegians overcoming the Law of Jante. This athlete not only pushed physical and mental boundaries but also stirred the nation, always with a twinkle in his eye and often embroiled in controversies. I'm referring to the man who would exclaim, "Child's play!" as he bested his competitors at the finish line: Petter Northug.

The Story of Petter

I'll never forget that moment. I was invited to deliver the opening keynote at the Harstad Conference, a premier business gathering in northern Norway. The lineup was diverse, ranging from a local influencer who had ascended to become "the most powerful media woman in Norway" to leading business figures and academics. Among them was one of Norway's most celebrated athletes: Petter Northug.

His name was synonymous with cross-country skiing dominance. Over the course of his illustrious career, Northug clinched 13 World Championship Gold medals and two Olympic Golds, setting numerous records in the process. But it wasn't just his athletic skills that set him apart; it was his larger-than-life personality. Known as one of the sport's fiercest competitors, Northug was celebrated for his dramatic finishes and unparalleled sprinting capabilities.

While the Swedes boasted of Zlatan Ibrahimović's soccer skills, his character would never fit the Norwegian mold. Petter Northug was "one of us."

Northug was not merely focused on defeating Sweden; he relished every opportunity to playfully mock them. His antics resonated with Norwegians and Swedes alike, echoing a rivalry rooted in generations. Northug was both admired and criticized for his audacious behavior and his confident—sometimes even cocky—remarks. This established him as a divisive figure in the skiing community. The combination of his unparalleled talent and undeniable charisma didn't make him an icon just in sports but also one of the major media personalities in Norway. Was he a superstar whose stature overshadowed the sport? Was Northug, by his sheer self-belief, challenging the ingrained Law of Jante? But on the chilly evening of January 20, 2020, prior to the Harstad Conference, there was a different Northug. VIPs and local politicians had gathered for a dinner. Northug and I were at separate tables. I observed a young man seemingly lost in his own world, a stark contrast to the assertive athlete who routinely defied norms and showcased his mastery in ways that were atypical for Norwegian athletes.

At dinner, Northug appeared distant, almost entirely engrossed in his phone. He seemed perpetually lost, endlessly scrolling through his Instagram feed, seemingly seeking dopamine hits from social media validation. While his body was there, his mind was far away.

I'm no psychiatrist, but I couldn't help reflecting on our encounter that evening. From media reports, I understood that Petter the Great, like many athletes nearing the end of their careers, struggled to maintain his once-peerless performance. Injuries and surging competition had challenged his dominance in the sport, culminating in his retirement in 2018—or at least, that was the public's understanding.

However, I see it differently. Northug, in my view, fell victim to the Law of Jante, and he never had the opportunity to conclude his career on his terms.

Petter Northug's path was fraught with challenges, primarily due to his clash with collective expectations. This was most evident in his relationship—or the evident lack of it—with the Norwegian Ski Federation (NSF). Northug frequently found himself at odds with Vidar Løfshus, the cross-country team's chief for a significant portion of his career. According to reports, their disagreements often centered on team participation and sponsorship matters. Northug, never one to bite his tongue, didn't hesitate to critique the NSF when he believed it was necessary. In return, NSF officials and coaches occasionally offered frank criticisms of Northug's choices and behaviors, further intensifying their publicized disputes.

The disputes between Northug and the NSF were multifaceted. They touched upon athlete autonomy, the commercialization of sports, and the dynamics of individual athletes within team structures. While many fans continued to adore Northug, these disagreements highlighted the inherent challenges faced by individuals in team environments, particularly when commercial stakes are high.

One major point of contention arose in 2013 when Northug signed a personal sponsorship agreement with the supermarket chain COOP. This move directly clashed with the interests of the team's primary sponsors. As a result, the NSF barred Northug from participating on the national team. But this disagreement was about more than just one deal. At its core was Northug's assertion that he should have the right to pursue personal sponsorships outside the team's jurisdiction. Conversely, Løfshus and the NSF believed in retaining control, arguing that sponsorship decisions should be made collectively rather than letting individual athletes supersede the established system.

It went as far as to instances when Northug wanted to participate in certain World Cup races but was not selected because of his nonparticipation in team activities or due to form considerations.

It may seem absurd, especially when considering how individual athletes in team sports like soccer or basketball manage personal sponsorship deals in addition to their team salaries. However, this was emblematic of the Norwegian national team's ethos. The bureaucratic framework was not just about ensuring the best equipment, training facilities, and logistics for the team. It was also a power play, reinforcing their influence and the importance of the collective spirit.

This discord exposed the rigidity of the existing system. Northug's battles heralded new deals and approaches that have since pushed the sport—which was direly in need of standout personalities, innovative strategies, and reinvestment—in fresh directions.

Northug personifies the spirit of competitive sports with his relentless pursuit of excellence, unforgettable moments of brilliance, and the inevitable highs and lows that define a champion's journey.

Yet, shadows marred Northug's illustrious career. He never truly got to be Petter the Great, facing hurdles not only at the onset but also toward the end of his cross-country career. It became evident that Northug wasn't cut out for legal wranglings and bureaucratic disputes; he yearned to shine. He thrived on the adrenaline rush from skiing battles, not courtroom skirmishes.

Constrained by these limitations, Northug was denied a fitting conclusion to his career. In today's context, athletes like soccer player Lionel Messi transcend their sport, benefiting both individually and contributing to the collective. Even pronounced individualists like Cristiano Ronaldo and Zlatan Ibrahimovic have enhanced the allure of soccer, lifting the stature of the entire sport. Northug was akin to a skiing dynasty, but the absence of freedom and support resulted in two major setbacks: for both Petter Northug himself and the sport of cross-country skiing, casting a shadow on the Norwegian Ski Federation.

After a particularly challenging period in his life, Northug crashed his car while intoxicated and fled the scene. This incident led to a 50-day jail sentence, which he served under an ankle monitor, coupled with extensive community service. This episode severely tarnished his public reputation, and Northug expressed profound regret for his behavior.

His journey—with its peaks and valleys—underscores the challenges of living under constant scrutiny. More critically, it highlights the detrimental effects of the Law of Jante, which has potentially stifled many gifted athletes over time.

Observing Northug that evening in 2020 evoked a sense of pity within me. He deserved a more fitting conclusion to his illustrious career. Perhaps it's this sentiment, even in the face of seemingly unforgivable actions, that can serve as a foundation. Once acknowledged and accepted, it can pave the way to an even stronger reintegration. Today, Northug has once again become "one of us," as the collective seems to have embraced his apologies and efforts to reclaim his life. While it's undeniable that Northug paid his dues, his story offers a vital lesson as we seek to understand the Viking Code.

Petter Northug, along with Magnus Carlsen and Suzann Pettersen, challenged boundaries. They sparked the search for belief in the Norwegian culture that it's possible to elevate individuals without compromising the strength of the collective. Recent success has even shown that, when values are aligned and rooted in high performance, the rise of an individual can uplift the entire collective.

Trust Thyself

"...Though one should trust oneself."

—Du skal tro at du er no!

Marcel and I, well acquainted with "Janteloven," or the Law of Jante, grapple with its constraints. Even now, in moments when I aspire to reach new heights, it feels like a weight pulling me down. It's become evident that self-doubt doesn't root us—it erodes us. Over time, I've pondered why certain individuals can navigate personal missteps with grace, while others falter. Why are some perceived as superficial, while others seem authentic? Why are some cast aside, while others are embraced by the collective?

Though I don't claim to have definitive answers, I surmise that those who appear most egocentric—despite potentially being the opposite—might just be revealing their insecurities. This perceived arrogance, perhaps a defense mechanism, inadvertently creates a barrier between them and the world around them. Marcel and I were having discussions on "Janteloven" during the Women's World Championship in Soccer. The Norwegian team, which, despite having world-class players from leading European clubs, failed to qualify for the next round. One notable decision was the sidelining of Barcelona's star player, Caroline Graham Hansen, in the decisive preliminary round match against Switzerland. When confronted by the media, Hansen's response came across as self-centered and inauthentic, and perhaps to many Norwegians, it felt like, "She is not one of us," especially as she seemed to challenge both the coach and the team. The disapproval in the next day's headlines was telling: "Janteloven står tydlig sterkt" (The Law of Jante evidently remains powerful). Subsequently, the national team's coach stepped down. Could this be another instance where the weight of the Law of Jante led to individual insecurity and therefore the fall of the collective?

Put differently, even though Hansen thrived and displayed creativity playing for Barcelona, could it be that she felt restricted and insecure within Norway's traditional framework? Did she lack the freedom and self-assurance to truly flourish? Rather than the public's perception of her as overconfident and egocentric, could it be the complete opposite? Was it not a surplus of confidence but a deficit of self-esteem that influenced her communication?

The lines distinguishing insecure bravado from genuine, deeply rooted self-trust may be faint from an external viewpoint. Yet, it appears to be a transformative period for Norwegian athletes in their relationship to self-confidence and trust. This foundational trust has been instrumental in their rise to global prominence, offering rich lessons for all to consider.

In the competitive realm of sports, where every millisecond or centimeter can mark the difference between victory and defeat, trust emerges as an invaluable yet intangible asset. While physical superiority, talent, and technique are undeniably vital, the athletic world is equally a mental arena. In this context, trust—both in oneself and in others—becomes the defining currency.

The Rise of the Individual

In Norwegian culture, transcending the Law of Jante hasn't meant forsaking societal values. Beneath this renewed embrace of self-belief remains an unwritten declaration of interdependence—*I am because you are.*

What has happened, though, is that Norway's top athletes have managed to harness their inner confidence while still holding onto the essence of their cultural identity. They have become embodiments of a new form of Norwegian individualism—one that does not rebel against the collective but rather complements it.

The meteoric rise of Suzann Pettersen, Magnus Carlsen, and Petter Northug, alongside the many Norwegian skiing champions, was seen as a source of national pride. Their individual achievements became a collective celebration, a symbol of what Norwegians can achieve when they believe in themselves and their potential.

By embracing individuality, these athletes have shown that it's possible to break free from societal constraints while still being deeply rooted in one's cultural identity. They've demonstrated that self-belief is a potent tool in the face of societal constraints. Every record they've broken, every podium reached, serves as a testament to the power of the individual spirit.

This individual spirit is not rebellious in nature; it's evolutionary. It doesn't overthrow the values of the Law of Jante; it redefines them in a contemporary context. The message is clear: you can be true to yourself, believe in your potential, and still be a proud product of your culture.

This empowerment through individuality carries a broader lesson for societies worldwide.

Cultures and traditions, as vital as they are for a nation's identity, should empower and not constrict. As the world becomes more interconnected and competitive, fostering an environment where individuals can believe in themselves becomes imperative. The Norwegian athlete's story serves as an inspirational lighthouse, signaling that it's possible to harmonize individual aspirations with collective values.

Marcel and I dedicated the day to delineating the essence of trust, examining its relationship to both high performance and values. We identified three pivotal elements that we believe have enabled Norwegians to transcend the limitations of the Law of Jante. These traits, we contend, form the bedrock of human growth. Marcel is firmly of the opinion that they serve as essential competencies and drivers for high performance in sports. Moreover, we both hold the conviction that these qualities can be nurtured, thereby enhancing intrinsic motivation, addressing extrinsic challenges, and fostering foundational values.

Self-trust: The Silent Rebellion

Every athlete encounters moments of doubt. Whether it's the pressure of a championship game, the daunting task of recovering from an injury, or the immense weight of national expectations, these moments can be paralyzing. For Norwegian athletes, the pervasive influence of the Law of Jante layers an additional challenge. When a cultural ethos continually suggests you shouldn't stand out, the journey toward recognizing and believing in one's unique capabilities becomes significantly profound.

However, the success of the modern Vikings is a testament to their deep-rooted self-trust. This isn't just about confidence in their athletic capabilities but a holistic belief in the journey, decisions, and path. Self-trust is a silent yet highly potent rebellion against the restrictive facets of the Law of Jante. Instead of capitulating to the idea that one shouldn't think they're special, these athletes have embraced their uniqueness, and it has been instrumental in their success.

Trust in Others: The Ripple Effect

The foundation of self-trust does not stand in isolation. It radiates throughout an athlete's ecosystem, fostering a deeper trust in teammates, coaches, support staff, and even fans. The principle is straightforward: when you trust in your own judgment, you naturally extend that trust to those you've chosen to surround yourself with. The manner in which you engage and behave can significantly influence others' perceptions of your self-confidence.

While self-trust and trust in others are intertwined, it is the depth of self-trust that often magnifies our capacity to trust others. Within such a trusting environment, collective growth is possible.

In team sports, this trust is the cornerstone of synergy and mutual understanding. When individual members place unwavering trust in their counterparts, the team functions as a unified entity.

Coaches also hold a pivotal role in this dynamic. Athletes entrust their careers to these guides, forging a symbiotic bond: while coaches rely on athletes to actualize strategies, athletes lean on their mentors for sound guidance. Witnessing this intricate web of trust, the broader Norwegian community becomes even more inspired, propagating an ever-expanding cycle of mutual trust.

Collective Trust: The Virtuous Cycle

The splendor of Norway's evolving ethos is that individual achievements no longer stand merely as lone pillars of success. Instead, they lay the bricks for a robust foundation, strengthening the nation's collective pride. When one athlete triumphs, it elevates the morale of the entire community. This shared exuberance and pride fortify societal ties, making them both adaptable and steadfast.

The narrative morphs from mere individual accomplishment to a tale of communal growth. Each medal, record, or accolade becomes a testament to the collective potential of Norwegians. This culture turns achievements into motivational touchstones, fueling others' aspirations. In this virtuous cycle, success begets success, with trust—in oneself and the collective—at its heart.

In the arena of Norwegian sports, trust has emerged as the transformative currency. This dual-faceted trust, both inward and outward, has paved the way for accomplishments that ripple far beyond the podium, touching the souls of communities and inspiring future generations.

The Power of Positive Reinforcement

One more aspect also seems to lie at the core of self-trust and stands strong in Norwegian culture. Amid the sweat, dedication, and tireless training of athletes, their mental state remains a delicate balance. Often, the difference between victory and defeat, or between perseverance and giving up, hinges on the power of positive reinforcement. One vital aspect that seems to underpin self-trust, and stands robustly in Norwegian culture, is the realization of the role played by an *encouraging ecosystem*. As the world of Norwegian sports has thrived, this understanding has equally grown.

The factor that Marcel and I believe to be essential for this development is the ability to *cheer for others*, to wish them well and uplift. We contend that this sentiment goes hand in hand with self-belief. Rooting for others, wishing them success, and even respecting the high-performance feats of competitors signify strength. It diminishes jealousy, fosters honest communication, and strengthens the foundation for collective growth.

Historically grounded in the tenets of the Law of Jante, Scandinavian societies, particularly Norway, have long prioritized collective harmony over individual accolades. This cultural emphasis raises a question: how can one applaud individual success without overshadowing the collective?

The answer lay in evolving the way Norwegians cheered and rooted for individual achievements, shifting from elevating one above the community to celebrating a member within it. Gradually, cheering for individual athletes morphed into a cultural norm. One can view cheering as a cultural evolution, contrary to the traditional Jante outlook yet harmoniously coexisting alongside it.

This cultural shift signified more than just vocal support; it marked a societal recognition of individual effort, dedication, and skill. By cheering, Norwegians were not just acknowledging an athlete's success, but the hard work, sacrifices, and challenges overcome to achieve it.

The significance of an encouraging shout, a supportive banner, or a cheering crowd can't be underestimated. For athletes, this support often translates into a tangible psychological boost.

Research has frequently shown that positive reinforcement can amplify motivation, increase resilience, and enhance performance. Athletes, knowing they have the backing of their peers and public, experience a surge in self-confidence and a reduction in performance anxiety. This support serves as a buffer against doubt, allowing athletes to focus more keenly on the task at hand.

Moreover, the knowledge that their successes are seen, recognized, and celebrated gives athletes an additional purpose. Beyond personal ambition, they now perform for their supporters, for those who believe in them. This symbiotic relationship between athletes and their supporters creates a powerful dynamic, propelling athletes to push boundaries further.

An essential part of the Viking Code is understanding that as individual athletes bask in their successes, a remarkable phenomenon unfolds. The lines between personal victory and collective achievement blur. A medal won by an athlete is a medal for Norway; a record broken is a record for the community.

This collective ownership of success ensures that the joy of accomplishments is widespread. Children look up to these athletes, drawing inspiration. Peers view them as benchmarks, pushing themselves harder. And for the broader community, every victory serves as a reminder of what's possible when talent meets dedication.

The virtuous cycle of achievements leading to encouragement, and vice versa, mirrors a reinforcement learning model. It fosters an environment where excellence is not just strived for but is expected, celebrated, and built upon.

Norway's shift toward positive reinforcement in sports underscores the universal power of encouragement. It's a testament to the idea that while individual brilliance can achieve greatness, collective support ensures that such greatness is sustained, celebrated, and serves as a strong foundation for future generations.

This ethos celebrates individual achievement while retaining the core value of community spirit. It's a paradigm where individual brilliance doesn't overshadow the collective but rather illuminates it.

In the pursuit of individual achievement, the essence of community should never be lost. The Norwegian athletic narrative offers a template: it's possible to shine as individuals while contributing to the collective. This balance ensures that as individuals rise, they lift the community with them. It's a delicate stride toward a dynamic equilibrium, ensuring that individual aspirations don't eclipse collective well-being. Individual ambition is not just tolerated; it is encouraged.

The first part of the Viking Code, therefore, teaches us that trust, both in oneself and the community, is foundational. It teaches us that success is a collective endeavor, with individual achievements adding to the shared experience of progress.

This first lesson in deciphering the Viking Code teaches us that a new generation of athletes has masterfully redefined the essence of the Law of Jante. By believing in themselves and their individual potential, they've paved a path of success not just for them but for the entire nation. Their journey underscores the importance of self-belief, emphasizing that true empowerment arises when individuality and culture walk hand in hand.

Marcel and I have identified clear benefits of emphasizing self-trust. Through our work, we have also come to realize the benefits both when it comes to building high-performance athletes and in building strong cultures rooted in solid values. Some of these reflections are what we want to take out of the first step of deciphering the Viking Code:

- **Decreased Projected Insecurities:** Individuals who lack self-trust often project their insecurities onto others. For example, individuals who frequently doubt their own integrity might readily question the integrity of others, even in the absence of evidence. This can be particularly problematic in team sports, leading to misunderstandings that create tension within the group. However, when you trust yourself—your instincts, feelings, and decisions—it provides a foundation for trusting others. Being confident in your own judgments naturally extends to having confidence in your assessments of others.

- **Authentic Relationships:** Self-trust leads to authenticity. When you are true to yourself, it becomes easier to be genuine with others. Authentic relationships are a fertile ground for mutual trust.

- **Responsibility for Decisions:** If you trust yourself, you take responsibility for your decisions, including whom you choose to trust. This means that instead of blaming others entirely for breaches of trust, you can reflect on your choices and learn from them.

- **Emotional Resilience:** Trusting oneself can lead to greater emotional resilience. This means that even if someone betrays your trust, you have the internal resources to cope, understand, and move on without it severely affecting your ability to trust again in the future.

- **Clear Boundaries:** Trusting yourself helps in establishing clear personal boundaries. When you know and respect your own limits, you can communicate them to others. This sets the stage for healthier relationships where trust can be built.

- **Ability to Assess Risks:** Trust isn't about believing that everyone is trustworthy. It's about assessing who is trustworthy and in what contexts. When you trust your own judgment, you can make better decisions about whom to trust and to what extent.

- **Enhanced Intuition:** Often, our gut feelings or intuitions play a role in trust. Trusting oneself enhances the ability to listen to and heed those intuitions, which can guide decisions about trusting others.

After decades of nurturing talent, Norway has evolved past the Law of Jante to a point where the best of both worlds—collective and individual achievements—have merged to create a unique cultural ethos.

Maintaining and evolving this legacy, which seamlessly integrates high performance with core values, is a task in itself. After the "genie was let out of the bottle," it has become crucial to constantly refine this dynamic balance. The importance of a dynamic approach, one that keeps progress in focus, is highlighted by the recurring, entrenched conflicts of the "old" world. Recent headlines from Norwegian media about Johannes Høsflot Klæbo, the cross-country skiing star and "Prince Charming," illustrate this point. On the one hand, he embodies the values of an exemplary human, while on the other, he is engaged in daily "battles" with the Norwegian Ski Federation. Then there's the young slalom sensation Lucas Braathen, who, despite media adoration, announced his withdrawal from the sport at the age of 23, after a 3-year dispute with the federation over branding rights had drained his passion for skiing.

A young man who, in recent years, has embodied this dynamic equilibrium to its fullest extent will conclude this first chapter of *The Viking Code*. He's a man who represents the transcendence of the Law of Jante while maintaining collective values like no other and someone who shows us how success and values at the pinnacle of the world are possible.

Karsten Warholm—Supertrust: "Values, When Something Is at Stake"

On July 1, 2021, in the heart of Norway, the athletics stadium in Oslo was a nexus of tension and fervor. The Diamond League, where aspirations simmer, is not just any track meet this year;

it's the preamble to the 2020 Summer Olympics, delayed courtesy of a global pandemic. The stands, though filled with a mosaic of international talent, have their gaze fixed on one local hero: Karsten Warholm. This young Norwegian hurdler isn't merely taking a lap in the 400-meter hurdles. For him, it's a dance of calibration, a prelude to an Olympian dream.

The din of the crowd is momentarily pierced by the speculative voice of the Norwegian commentator, musing about Warholm's preparedness. The eyes of those gathered are inexorably drawn to the track, as each athlete locks into position. Among them, on his favored seventh track, stands Warholm, almost exuding a tangible aura. For him, this isn't just a race; it's a testament. His eyes, pools of raw determination, send an unspoken challenge to every spectator. And then, breaking the mounting tension, a robust "Come on!"—a battle cry signaling to the world that he isn't just there to participate. He's there to dominate. As the gun's report slices through the air, the race begins.

"Det er ny verdensrekord, Karsten fra det norske havgapet løper fortere enn det noensinne har blir gjort. . . . Det skulle ikke være mulig for en nordmann?" the voice from the Norwegian broadcaster NRK1 reverberates with a mix of shock and admiration. Translated, the disbelief is palpable: "It's a new world record. Karsten, emerging from the cradle of the Norwegian Sea, has just done the unthinkable. . . . How can this be possible for a Norwegian?" For a fleeting moment, the stadium is cocooned in stunned silence. Then, like a dam breaking, a wave of applause crashes down, each clap a tribute to the man of the hour.

In the sweltering humidity of Tokyo, just over a month after his monumental feat in Oslo, Warholm again toed the starting line. The Olympic Stadium, an architectural marvel, now bore witness to a different kind of artistry—one of human potential. There he was, now in lane six, encircled by a cadre of formidable athletes who would, in mere minutes, collectively produce an unprecedented spectacle in the 400-meter hurdles.

And then, in what felt like a blink, Warholm had again redefined what was humanly possible. Clocking 45.94 seconds, he had shaved an astonishing 76 hundredths of a second off a record he had only just set. It wasn't just a triumph; it was a paradigm shift.

Switzerland's *Neue Zürcher Zeitung* newspaper, capturing the collective astonishment of the world, ran a simple yet profound headline: "How is this possible?" It went on to articulate a sentiment shared by many: "Never before in athletics had there been such a quantum leap at the pinnacle of performance." Theories abounded—cutting-edge shoes, superior tracks. But these seemed inadequate explanations for the magnitude of the feat.

Some records in sports are etched in popular memory: Usain Bolt's lightning-fast 9.58 seconds in the 100 meters, or Bob Beamon's seemingly endless 8.90-meter long jump. Both were moments that made us question the boundaries of human achievement. Yet, Warholm's 45.94 seconds felt otherworldly, as if he had momentarily escaped Earth's gravitational pull and raced in the ethereal confines of the moon.

Karsten Warholm often jests, with a twinkle in his eye, that he might have been over-served when self-confidence was being handed out at birth. Yet, this isn't hubris unchecked. His robust ego is anchored by an equanimity that allows him to navigate both the intoxicating highs of victory and the rare troughs of defeat. This blend of audacious self-belief, balanced with a surprising lightness of being, is what colors his persona. With his third world champion title since 2017, his 2023 race showed the world his dominance: he is the heroic hustler of hurdles.

Embedded in Warholm's journey is an ethos that's disarmingly simple: diligence paired with joy. Committing to a staggering 1,200 hours of training annually, he embodies the idea that true success is birthed from volition.

The man behind the success is Leif Olav Alness—a figure who could easily be the eccentric, time-travel obsessed Doc Brown of

Back to the Future. Originating from the modest Norwegian town of Torvikbukt and later immersing himself in the world of biomechanics in Oslo, Alness emerged as Warholm's coaching maestro. Their dynamic? A juxtaposition of a septuagenarian, obsessed with the mastery of movement, and a vivacious 27-year-old, ever the maverick. It's a collaboration of a biohacker and a joker, culminating in an athletic narrative for the ages.

The unorthodox duo of Alness and Warholm enjoy taking the public behind the scenes. The world is privy to their idiosyncrasies: the hijinks of film pistol competitions in cramped apartments, the comical image of Warholm propelled on a luggage cart through hotel lobbies, the shared moments of stillness while fishing. Their dynamic transcends the traditional boundaries of athlete and coach. Warholm likens their souls to a paradoxical dance—his being old in the frame of a young man, while Alness' vibrancy is enshrouded by the years.

However, as the adage goes, when it's game time, it's pain time. Beneath their shared laughter lies a palpable intensity, a metamorphosis that occurs when training morphs into competition mode. The joviality recedes, replaced by the fierce, raw hunger for excellence. Warholm's approach to competition is nothing short of a spectacle: screams that echo the arenas, self-inflicted slaps that jolt him to life, and expletives that seem to coax his body to stretch beyond its limits. Far from mere gimmicks, these have evolved into an adrenaline-releasing arsenal for Warholm, a ritualistic dance before the storm.

Warholm hasn't just participated in the 400-meter hurdles. He's reinvented it. Where convention dictated a steady build-up, Warholm introduced the temerity of a sprinter. His philosophy is grounded in the knowledge that in elite races, the final moments aren't for clawing back time but for holding the fortress. His audacious approach isn't just about personal milestones; it's a clarion call that pushes his adversaries to elevate their game.

But Warholm symbolizes not only individual success but, more importantly, the collective ethos embedded in the Viking Code. Like no other, he understands the significance of participating in small communities. His home club, Dimna IL, located on the tiny island of Dimnøya with just 1,398 residents, receives his regular support. He founded the Karsten Warholm Invitational, an annual indoor competition held in the local hall in Ulsteinvik. Each year, a thousand spectators fill the hall to witness invited international stars up close, while local and national athletes get the chance to compete against these global giants. It's the environment, the grassroots sport, and the voluntary commitment of parents that matter. It's his homeland— Norway—and the deep-rooted cultural ethos there. Warholm brings the gold back to Norway and is celebrated everywhere as "one of us."

At a prestigious gathering in 2019, the Norwegian sports community awarded Warholm the "Role Model of the Year" for his integration work and his commitment beyond the sport. Observers in the room didn't merely see a top-tier athlete. Instead, they witnessed an ethos come alive—an ethos built on compassion, engagement, and an innate sense of community. Sarah Louise Rung and Aksel Lund Svindal, the evening's eloquent speakers, remarked on the impossible task of pinning a flaw on him:

> He genuinely cares about his fellow human beings, is a likable competitor, and is kind and open to everyone. The Role Model of the Year is a cheerful guy; he truly is a happy salmon from the outskirts of Norway. He always finds time for young people and values volunteer work. It's no easy task to be a global star and simultaneously maintain a positive image, but Karsten Warholm masters this in a fantastically delicate manner. The jury eagerly searched for negative aspects of the

candidate, but the only thing they found was that he tends to arrive a bit late for training. He is a likable guy and clearly embodies the good values he received from his family and his origins in Ulsteinvik.

Before he won the award, Warholm had sat down with the Norwegian Athletics Federation to be interviewed on the topic of core values:

If we are tolerant, I believe we can go very far. It's important to me to use my influence in a positive way, which means declining offers and obligations that contradict my values. The special thing about values is that they often don't mean much until something is really at stake, and that's what I want to demonstrate. I want to prove that I stand up for my values, even when there's resistance and times are tough.

Warholm can be seen as a rare specimen of an athlete—one who not only achieves extraordinary performances on the track but also embodies strong values that resonate with people in all walks of life. He is the most explosive runner and, at the same time, one of the friendliest and most relaxed people.

He embodies what we will come to understand as the Viking Code, which combines fierce determination with a commitment to values. Warholm is a testament to the idea that integrity and top-tier performance aren't mutually exclusive. He's proof that you can shatter records with a heart full of principles and a face adorned with a smile.

On June 15, 2023, in the echoing vastness of the Bislett Games stadium, the atmosphere was one of reverence. Warholm stood there, not as a fleeting star of the moment but as a living legend. David McCarthy, the evening's last scribe, encapsulated the sentiment with a simple yet profound observation: "These Norwegian lads, they're sound."

2

Unleashing the Uncatchables: The Head-start Advantage

AMID THE BOUNDLESS horizons of human ambition, secret is known to those who've touched the pinnacle of greatness. *It's the magic of starting early*—a potent nudge propelling dreamers on a journey to become the *uncatchables*.

Think about it.

Isn't it often the simplest truths that hold the most profound wisdom? The gentle yet compelling allure of early immersion in one's chosen realm acts not merely as a stepping stone, but as the very catalyst of excellence.

Various thinkers and scholars have delved into the mysteries of this early advantage. Starting young, it seems, isn't merely about having extra time; it's about catching the winds of youth when the sails of talent are at their most responsive.

In *The Talent Code*, Daniel Coyle paints a fascinating tableau of science that explains the magic of early beginnings. The tender tendrils of a child's brain are like sponges, eager and open, making childhood a time rife for swift skill acquisition. It is like pouring water into the fertile soil of a young mind. Early experiences aren't just droplets; they are the rain that cultivates mastery.

But where did that come from?

I turn to Marcel for an obvious and simple reference point to get our discussion around the "uncatchables" going. In the realm of success literature, Malcolm Gladwell's *Outliers* stands as a monumental work, illuminating the factors that contribute to high levels of success. In Gladwell's magnum opus, rather than merely glorifying innate talent, he pushes the envelope by exploring the environment, opportunities, cultural background, and sheer practice hours behind iconic success stories. The crux of his argument is the renowned "10,000-hour rule," suggesting that it takes approximately 10,000 hours of dedicated practice to achieve mastery in any field. However, critics argue that this concept overly simplifies the journey to expertise or is "a provocative generalization," according to Anders Ericsson. Ericsson's research on expert musicians cites that not everyone with 10,000 hours under their belt becomes a master, and not all masters necessarily clocked in those hours. "The 10,000 Hour Rule: Catchy and easy to remember, but on some pretty shaky scientific footing," Ericsson argues.

Gladwell's perspective highlights the role of systemic factors in personal achievements, but it also reminds us that while practice is crucial, the context in which it occurs can be equally, if not more, significant. *Outliers* aims at having the reader reconsider the isolated narratives of genius and prodigy, revealing a broader landscape of success, wherein time, place, culture, and opportunity dance in harmony propelling what has famously been recognized as the outliers.

When you start exploring the Viking Code, it can initially seem much like Marcel's coltsfoot analogy. You never know where the next one will crack, and it is hard to see the winning formula. But once you look under the surface and see the cracks in the pavement, you will find the ingredients of this Norwegian success formula as the underlying principles become apparent.

Take Marit Bjørgen, for instance. She personifies the ideal Norwegian skiing hero: unpretentious, straightforward, and deeply rooted in traditional values. In the age of social media and the attention economy, many might see her demeanor as unremarkable, even dull. Yet, when she speaks, her words carry weight. Her quiet strength and humble origins resonate with many Norwegians. Characteristics often associated with Marit include her grounded nature and appreciation for life's simplicities.

Her upbringing, which some might deem ordinary, mirrors countless childhoods in Norway and epitomizes the values of the Viking Code. Growing up alongside multiple generations on a farm, everyone played a part. "Strong as a bear and kind to everyone" was a descriptor in her biography, *A Winner's Heart: The Marit Bjørgen Story*. Her early life was steeped in physical activity: sawing, stacking firewood, hunting, haymaking, and an early cup of coffee for everyone. Her parents both had athletic backgrounds, providing Marit and her brother with a diverse range of physical challenges. This foundation made her physically superior to her peers, setting her on a path to national prominence.

Norwegian sports would also not be without "Ildsjeler" (fire souls). Idar Terje Belsvik was this person in Marit's life and provided the good skis—even though they did not have the resources like the athletes from the big cities—and without Terje, Marit's journey might have looked vastly different. She balanced the camaraderie of team sports like handball with the individual challenges of skiing, creating a harmonious blend in her athletic pursuits.

Marit Bjørgen is emblematic of many facets integral to the Viking Code. Marcel points out an interesting aspect that despite her impressive physical foundation, Marit wasn't conventionally suited for endurance sports; she has too many (large) muscles for cross-country skiing. Marcel makes another interesting point that with her upbringing and background she could have been even more suited for an even more popular sport discipline, and she might have made it even further. But this head-start advantage in cross-country skiing made Marit "uncatchable." When she retired in 2018, Marit Bjørgen stood as the greatest winter Olympian of all time. She had earned 8 Olympic gold medals, 18 World Championship golds, and 25 Norwegian Championship golds.

The Symphony of Athletic Development

I recall recounting to Marcel a tale from my own life—of my early days in endurance training. With an almost manic fervor, I'd push myself to lead in the initial lap, establishing a lead that felt like an insurmountable chasm. And once ahead, the game was simple: maintain the lead, no matter what. This wasn't just about the thrill of the race; it was a metaphor for life, for staying ahead, for being uncatchable.

I can almost see the cogs turning in Marcel's mind, the gears grinding as he sifts through years of knowledge, training science, and the intricacies of the human psyche. "Training tears down, relaxation and nutrition build up," he muses, a contemplative expression on his face. "Muscles are stupid; they do as they're commanded," he continues, trying to stress a point—dissuading the recklessness of pushing oneself beyond limits without purpose.

There's a certain irony, I thought. Here I am, a grown man, with these seemingly hardwired notions about training, trying to lead a conversation where I should have been a student. As I had begun traversing down my monologue, eager to showcase what I knew, Marcel intervened with the grace of a maestro steering an orchestra.

"I'm quite partial to LTAD," he says, breaking my train of thought. And suddenly, I find myself back in my uncomfortable comfort zone—like a sponge ready to absorb, to learn from some-one with depths of knowledge that I had yet to fathom.

Isn't it peculiar? We often forget the simple wisdom that our two ears and single mouth might be hinting at: the virtue of lis-tening twice as much as we speak. With a tinge of humility, I admit to myself I'm clueless about what Marcel refers to. Trying to keep up, I mentally note, *long-term athlete development (LTAD)*.

"Visualize a nine-year-old stepping onto a soccer field. At which development stage is he?" Marcel poses. I stay silent, sens-ing he's about to weave a narrative. "He isn't just a boy, and this isn't merely practice. He's in a beautifully orchestrated movement dance, led by a maestro known as the coach." This child is unknow-ingly at the threshold of the LTAD stages—a potential pathway that could crown him an "uncatchable" in the arena of sports.

Australian sports scientist Kelvin Giles coined the term *long-term athlete development* and pioneered its principles in the 1980s. Giles implemented LTAD in national sports programs in Australia during the 1980s and 1990s. In the late 1990s, Canadian scientist Richard Way helped popularize LTAD principles, leading to adoption in Canada.

What started as a local methodology is today a globally recognized model for talent development. It's a manifesto for fostering sport, promoting health, and sculpting achievement.

By the 2000s, LTAD was being implemented and heavily used by Istvan Balyi and Canadian Sport for Life. With the LTAD methodology, observations, research, and introspection soon helped coaches around the world recognize that their traditional athlete-grooming methods were akin to using a blunt axe—ineffective and potentially damaging. And from this realization, the LTAD has been sharpened and globally promoted, a blue-print Marcel revered.

Today, LTAD guides the systematic evolution of athletes. It professes a simple truth: athletes grow in phases, and each phase has a unique set of needs and characteristics.

LTAD's ultimate mission? To delineate a lucid journey for athletes, offering them apt training, competition, and recovery tailored to their developmental milestones. It's a compass pointing toward maximizing potential and evading pitfalls like overtraining, burnout, or injury.

LTAD: Mapping the Athlete's Odyssey

The first stage of LTAD is known as *Active Start*. From the moment of birth to the tender age of 6, the world is a vast playground. Here, through frolic and active play, the seeds of fundamental motor skills are sown. Like the strings of a harp, each skill resonates with the child's sense of accomplishment and mastery. During this phase, as the mind races with growth, the young synapses are hard at work. They construct the neural infrastructure that, in the future, would be the very highways of talent development. It's a stage replete with magic—where tongues find words, palates discover tastes, and tiny feet and hands grasp the wonders of motion.

As these tiny wonders navigate their world, they intertwine play with learning—where muscles learn to converse with the mind. In this haven of exploration, risk is met with curiosity, and the world is perceived with all senses wide awake.

But this is just the prologue.

What follows is known as *FUNdamentals*. A stage reserved for children aged 6–8, where fun fuses with both discipline and freedom. This isn't about soccer goals or basketball hoops; it's about the sheer joy of movement—jumping, sprinting, and balancing. The children stand on the threshold of what is poetically coined the Motorical Golden Age. Here, they learn the subtle arts that would one day make them wizards on fields and courts. The teachings of a tennis ball's flight, or the rhythm of a bouncing basketball, can carve paths of mastery in many a sport. Vision, strategy, and timing are woven into the fabric of their play, with multitudes of sports painting their canvas.

As the journey progresses, children aged 8–11 for girls and 9–12 for boys set foot on the *Learn to Train* plateau. The seeds sown in previous stages now blossom into a deeper understanding of rules, tactics, and refined skills. They revel in diverse sports that enrich them with laughter, challenges, and camaraderie. This is where sparks of potential catch fire. Yet, the balance of free play with structured training remains sacred.

The *Train to Train* phase—for girls aged 11–15 and boys 12–16—signifies a metamorphosis. Specialized training takes precedence, honing skills, tactics, and the physique. Marcel, with his infectious enthusiasm, weaves in a tale of Manchester United's Academy shared to him from the legendary Ole Gunnar Solskjær. The Manchester United Academy wasn't about creating robotic players and early specialization but nurturing individual brilliance. The academy embraced the LTAD's principles, safeguarding the flame of passion from the gusts of burnout or injury, consistently ranking as the most productive in England for the last 10 years, according to the Premier League. Solskjær told how they used to move the parents away from the field in order to let the kids practice what they had trained during the games in order to emphasize the development—train to train—over winning.

LTAD: To Specialize or Not to Specialize

My thoughts drifts off to a recent conversation with my child-hood friend, Krister. As we recounted memories of indulging in multiple sports until our mid-teens, he shared how his 13-year-old son was now part of an elite ice hockey training regimen. This took me down a familiar memory lane, with Gladwell's *Outliers* in the backdrop. The book takes a closer look at the "Matthew

Effect," highlighting a poignant insight from the Gospel of Matthew:

> For unto everyone that hath shall be given, and he shall have abundance. But from him that hath not shall be taken away even that which he hath. (Matthew 25:29)

As Gladwell's pen danced on paper, he noted how success breeds opportunities, which further fuel success. However, he also underscored a tragic oversight in talent selection, where birth months could overshadow sheer potential, leading to a massive loss in unrecognized and untapped talent.

Gladwell astutely observes, "Success is not just about innate ability. It's combined with a number of key factors such as opportunity, meaningful hard work, and your cultural legacy." In the beginning of the book he starts off pointing at the Czech Republic's soccer team roster. The absence of players born in the latter months—July through December—is glaring. Essentially, the potential of half of the Czech's athletic talent pool had been overlooked or prematurely discarded simply based on the fact that the early selection and specialization had left out "late bloomers" and the mere fact that at this early age one year of development has immense impact on not only the physical structure, but also the general motor development of kids. For those fortunate enough to be born earlier in the year, the developmental gap, even if it's just a few months, could mean a ticket to an elite academy. Such institutions are laden with resources, top-tier coaching, and intensive training.

Marcel contends that during the critical phase of specialization, the system might unintentionally overlook late bloomers. He connects this oversight to the relative age effects (RAEs), which highlight the disparities between athletes born in the same selection year. Such disparities can lead to higher dropout rates and diminish the talent pool across various sports. A study interviewing seven talent development experts explored the nuances of RAEs. It emphasized the importance of educating stakeholders and adjusting the development environment, such as implementing delayed selections and focusing on skills. This leads to a thought-provoking question: How many budding talents, similar to a young, undeveloped Lionel Messi, have we lost to these early selection processes?

Between the ages of 15 and 23, the mantra of LTAD becomes *Train to Compete*. Those honed-in elite academies, now with their initial advantage, if nurtured rightly, evolve into the "uncatchables." This isn't just a protocol; it's a meticulously crafted framework. There are nuances, of course, dependent on the sport, gender differences, and the individual pace at which adolescents hit puberty. Here, athletes sharpen their sport-specific acumen, gearing up for stellar performances. This is the moment when emerging talents break the mold and step onto the global stage. With intensified physical, technical, and emotional training, they morph into full-time athletes, competing both nationally and internationally. This phase demands unwavering commitment. The training's volume and intensity hover on the precipice of one's potential. Athletes are subjected to diverse competitive conditions, and their recovery and mental resilience are meticulously calibrated. Some even discover profound capabilities that propel them into entirely new disciplines.

The *Train to Win* phase, generally assigned to athletes aged 19 and older, shifts the lens toward peak performance in elite competitions. Here, one would typically find athletes competing in eminent tournaments like the Olympics or World Championships. Training becomes increasingly personalized, with an acute emphasis on physical conditioning and psychological fortitude. This phase has evolved into a relentless pursuit of excellence, underpinned by science and technology. Athletes are enmeshed in a rigorous regimen, with every aspect of their training, recovery, and mental well-being continuously monitored and fine-tuned to preclude injuries or burnouts.

Then there's the *Active for Life* phase. Accessible at any age, its essence lies in promoting sustained physical activity, irrespective of competitive ambition. It's about embracing sports as a means of recreation, wellness, and camaraderie. One can choose to remain Fit for Life or persist with the spirit of competition as *Competitive for Life*. This phase encapsulates both structured and spontaneous activities, encouraging various roles, from coaching to volunteering.

The Canadian LTAD model has garnered global admiration, credited for fostering holistic athlete development, curtailing injuries, and boosting lifelong sports participation. However, it mandates a concerted endeavor from sports entities, mentors, guardians, and all associated players.

Yet, what's the Viking Code's unique touchpoint?

How did an entire generation of Norwegian athletes seize this "head-start advantage" and ascend as the uncatchables?

The Norwegian Way: Get Up, Get Out, and Move

Marcel and I discerned that the structured developmental arc was inherently rooted in Norwegian culture, even before Canada codified LTAD. Beyond Canada's structured model, Norway exhibited a similar ethos, albeit in a more organic, nonschematic manner.

Norway's vast countryside isn't just about its grandiose facilities. It's about their purposeful use. Norway's cultural heartbeat resonated with an age-old ethos of holistic movement. Way before the concept of systematically sculpting world-class athletes took root, Norwegians prioritized all-rounded physicality. It wasn't confined to elite urban academies. Rural landscapes echoed the same ethos: "Get up, get out, and move." This intrinsic bond with nature and an ingrained habit of immersing oneself in the outdoors was Norway's precursor to LTAD. It wasn't merely an athletic blueprint; it was a life-affirming roadmap.

Norway underscored the significance of holistic athleticism, or as termed in its native lexicon, "Breddeidrett." As with many of us growing up in this culture, our engagement wasn't limited to just one sport. Whether it was soccer, biathlon, or skiing, our pursuits shaped us into versatile athletes. This diverse exposure not only laid a robust foundation for our athletic endeavors but also primed us for the ever-evolving contours of our respective sports. Foreseeing the future trajectory of any sport is speculative at best. Yet, the versatility imbibed from this broad-based approach equipped us for whatever changes lay ahead.

Marcel and I agree that embracing a more expansive approach not only hones a richer skill set but also minimizes injuries during pivotal developmental phases. Interestingly, in the countryside, this wasn't a conscious strategy but rather a logistical necessity. For a team to exist, every member had to be versatile, participating in "Breddeidrett" to maintain a complete roster. This isn't a universal phenomenon in Norway, but in many regions, it remains true. Growing up in quaint locales, like my hometown of Røros, often meant diversifying one's athletic repertoire. It ensured the team's continuity and sometimes even demanded filling in different roles if teammates were sidelined due to illness or absences. It's crucial to discern that this wasn't a structured plan. Understanding its implications is key, as development isn't a monolithic process. Adopting an early selection process and creating elite academies risks overlooking latent talents. In sprawling metropolises, though even Oslo leans more toward a village in its dynamics, the Matthew Effect is subtler, given the vast talent pool and nuanced selection criteria.

Reverting to our initial focus areas, many countries, particularly smaller ones, have grappled with the challenges of athlete development. Today's performance cultures, in their eagerness to harness young talent, tend to funnel them into intensive, sport-specific regimens. This approach often results in premature burn-out, injuries in subsequent growth stages, and the unfortunate oversight of potential late bloomers. Consider Erling Haaland, for instance. Had he been appraised solely on his skills at age 12, would he have aligned with Barcelona's meticulous selection for their "tiki-taka" soccer style?

Norway's nuanced approach, the Viking Code, has indeed been groundbreaking, but it comes with a caveat for those eager to replicate it abroad. Norway's organic integration of LTAD principles stands as an emblem of its unwavering dedication to nurturing potential. It's a lesson for the world: spotting talent is just the inception; the real journey is about fostering, refining, and elevating it. And maybe, in this journey, you unveil those rare gems, the ones predestined to lead.

Before delving into global best practices, it's pivotal to intro-spect, understand one's distinctive patterns, and comprehend their progress. A salient element of early development in the Viking Code reveals a profound truth ingrained in Norwegian culture: As parents, it's deemed irresponsible not to foster the physical development of one's children. In essence, it's a call to: *Get Out. Get Up. And Move.*

Erling Haaland: The Rise of the Uncatchable

Every era of sport has transformative moments. These moments captivate and redefine what we believe to be possible. They make us pause, reflect, and utter in awe, "How did we not see this coming?"

I remember the long journeys back from my own away games, the unspoken rivalries and teasing with my teammates and the numerous distractions in everyday life or even at night when we couldn't sleep. One was the FIFA soccer video game, a virtual companion for countless soccer enthusiasts, including myself. But as with all things, eras shift, and the world moves forward. After selling an astounding 350 million copies, FIFA passed the torch to its successor: Electronic Arts. And as if heralding this new age, the face on its cover of the EA Sports FC 24 game box isn't one from soccer meccas like Brazil, Argentina, or Spain. Instead, we find a striking figure from Norway. He's a blond, imposing figure, reminiscent of the legendary Vikings. His name? Erling Haaland.

But dispel any notions of a fierce Viking warrior, navigating the tumultuous seas and conquering lands. This is a tale of a young man, hailing from the quaint town of Bryne—barely a speck on the vast map with its modest population of 12,000. And yet, from this unlikely place, Haaland emerges, not with a warrior's cry, but with an infectious grin, driven by a deceptively simple mission: to find the net, time and time again. Erling Haaland was born to score goals.

The city of Leeds, his birthplace, could've celebrated him as the crown jewel of soccer. Yet, Norway was his chosen path, and in doing so, he gave the world a sports narrative it didn't know it needed. The arc of Haaland's ascent in the soccer realm wasn't a prolonged one; it was meteoric. Playing with the older boys, he joined the youth academy of his hometown Bryne at age five. And when most teenagers are navigating the anxieties of high school, he was making his mark in the professional league, debuting for his hometown team Bryne at just 15. But Haaland was not only a soccer talent. With an impressive repertoire spanning 14 titles across handball, athletics, and even cross-country skiing, the world might have known him as one of the world's leading handball players or perhaps as an Olympic decathlete.

By 17, Haaland had moved on to Norway's leading soccer club, Molde. Having "eaten like a horse" and grown 7 centimeters

(2.75 inches) in just one year, Haaland emerged as a towering presence on the pitch against rival Brann in Bergen. He achieved what seemed like the impossible: four goals, all within the opening 20 minutes. On May 30, 2019, barely an adult at 18, he orchestrated a symphony of goals, a staggering nine in a single match, leading Norway to a 12-0 triumph over Honduras during the FIFA U-20 World Cup.

The picturesque Austrian city of Salzburg would be the backdrop for his next act. Having joined the ranks of Red Bull Salzburg at the dawn of 2019, the stage was set. The prodigious striker didn't just adapt; he thrived, evolving with every match. The Champions League, often regarded as the zenith of club soccer, bore witness to this Norwegian phenom's brilliance. And true to his burgeoning legend, Haaland announced his arrival with a hat trick on his debut, signaling to the world that here was a talent that defied norms.

Few would argue that choosing Borussia Dortmund was a calculated decision for Haaland's next move. The Bundesliga, with its inherent celebration of attacking soccer, coupled with Dortmund's penchant for lightning-fast, aggressive gameplay, seemed tailor-made for Haaland's predatory style. Many pundits waited with bated breath, skeptical, perhaps expecting the pressure to be too immense, the stage too large. Yet, Haaland's unparalleled knack for locating the back of the net and scaling newer challenges silenced his naysayers, one goal at a time.

In Salzburg, they fondly remembered him, noting, "He spreads good vibes when you are around him." His Bundesliga debut? An affirmation in the form of a hat trick.

Then, the narrative shifted. The curtain rose on Pep Guardiola, the orchestrator of "tiki-taka." This strategy, on paper, seemed to favor the nimble and the nuanced over the physically imposing. As Haaland merged into the fabric of what many hailed as soccer's best team in history, the question arose again: Could he adjust? Could he shine among the stars? The conclusion was unequivocal. By season's end, the 22-year-old Norwegian had not only etched himself as the face of the present but had lifted Manchester City to global supremacy. A treble—the League, the Cup, the Champions League—all punctuated by Haaland's mind-boggling 52 goals in 50 appearances. History books were rewritten every weekend. The statistics spoke volumes—three hat tricks in his opening eight games, 30 goals in a mere 25 UCL outings, shattering records faster than even luminaries like Ronaldo or Messi in their nascent years. And in a staggering performance against Leipzig, he left an indelible mark with five goals in a 57-minute spectacle.

So, what drives Erling Haaland? It's simple. Relentless hard work.

In the complex skill set needed in professional soccer, certain threads stand out—not because of their glitz, but because of their texture. Erling Haaland's discipline, commitment, and unique persona are such threads. Eirik Hestad, a former colleague, once succinctly remarked about Haaland, "It's just who he is." While many laud his dedication and even liken his discipline and diet to that of Ronaldo's, it's the testimonies of those close to him that best describes his character. Take, for instance, the words of Pep Guardiola, a man who has orchestrated symphonies with some of soccer's greatest maestros. Even he admits to rarely having seen a professional with Haaland's caliber. The viral image of Haaland sporting sleep caps and nasal bandages, honing his breathing during sleep, speaks volumes of his commitment. Around him, there's an electric charge—from physios to fledgling teammates, all are inspired to elevate their craft. But what distinguishes Haaland from other superstars like Mbappe and Neymar is a trait often overlooked in this age of individualism—selflessness. Despite his monumental goal tally, he's not hesitant to trust the collective, to play that crucial pass, believing that the team's triumph will amplify his personal glory.

One of these special moments is a testament to this character that unfolded on May 6, 2023. Manchester City, with the league title within reach, were dictating the narrative at the Etihad Stadium. With a 2-0 lead, mostly thanks to German midfielder Ilkay Gündogan's brace, having scored both goals, the scene seemed set for a routine win. Then a penalty was awarded, offering Haaland a tantalizing chance to add to his legendary tally and so seal the victory. But in an act that stunned spectators, he handed the ball to Gündogan. The older player, momentarily baffled, questioned Haaland's intent. With Haaland's gentle insistence and perhaps touched by the magnanimity, Gündogan stepped up. But soccer is fickle, and his shot missed its mark. Guardiola's fury was evident. A seemingly comfortable lead was now perilously close to slipping away when Leeds retaliated with a goal. As the final whistle blew, sealing City's narrow victory, Guardiola's first act was to admonish Haaland with a fervent directive: "You always take it!" Yet, in that gesture, amid the tumult of a game, the essence of Haaland was clear—a gesture from a personality who, in a world where personal accolades often eclipse team spirit, chose the path less traveled as he wanted to reward his teammate with a hat trick.

When we think of soccer stars at this level, we often envision memorable goals, acrobatic saves, or magic touches. Yet, Erling Haaland's journey to soccer stardom offers a broader mix of achievements that goes beyond the soccer pitch. The foundation was laid early: At just 5, young Haaland set a world long-jumping record. As a teen, during a sprint for Dortmund, his pace was so swift it could have earned him a berth in the World Championships for the 60-meter dash. Off the pitch, his sense of rhythm isn't just limited to outpacing defenders. With his "Flow King" rap, his YouTube video now has more than 9 million views. Haaland has become a cultural phenomenon. His signature post-goal celebration, both playful and iconic, has become the yardstick of aspiration for budding soccer players worldwide—even influencing toddlers like my neighbor's three-year-old.

In many ways, Haaland is a manifestation of genetic perfection and cultivated passion. His mother, an accomplished heptathlete, passed down her athletic genes. Meanwhile, his father's fervor for soccer ignited Haaland's own burning love for the game. But while genetics might provide the blueprint, it is Haaland's determination and environment that molded the player we see today.

The trajectory of Haaland's career isn't just the arc of a shooting star, but a masterclass in timing and choice. His transitions from one club to another always seemed to align with his personal growth trajectory, a testament to his ability to be in sync with his career's rhythm. A crucial aspect of his success is the sheer consistency of his goal-scoring. It's as if every time he steps onto the field, he's on a singular mission—to find the net.

But beneath the spotlight, it's the unseen hours that make the difference. In the saga of Erling Haaland, we don't just see a soccer player; we witness the evolution of an individual who, by every measure, is dedicated to the craft of perfection. An uncatchable team-player with a big smile on his face licensed to score goals.

3

Success Is Voluntary; Talent Can Be Found Everywhere

SINCE THE DAYS when Vikings ventured onto the vast, seemingly endless sea, believing the world was flat, coastal Norwegians have possessed a unique spark. We often romanticize islanders for their zest for life, their dances, and their songs. But what of those who dwelt by the rugged coastlines?

For those residing along Norway's extensive 100,915 kilometers (62,705 miles) of coast, a consistent principle has resonated throughout generations: work hard, forge alliances, and thrive. While the "frozen" inlanders faced their own set of challenges, the tales of the coastal inhabitants tell a distinct narrative.

Our ancestors crafted boats. But not just any boats—they built open vessels that braved the unknown. Their adventurous spirit recognized no limits. They weren't deterred by setbacks; indeed, *they failed, therefore they succeeded.*

Take the story of Naddodd, a refugee Norseman, who set sail for the Faroe Islands, only to find himself lost on the shores of what we now recognize as Iceland. In his quest for signs of life, he climbed a mountain searching for fire. Finding none, he left.

49

As snow began to fall during his journey home, he christened the place Snæland, or Snowland. Through sheer serendipity, he discovered a new land.

He was like Leif "The Lucky One" Erikson, who half a millennium before Columbus, might have been the first European to step onto American shores. One can almost hear the exchanges among his crew, a blend of enthusiasm, uncertainty, and sheer audacity, echoing from the shores of the Norwegian coast along the lines of:

"Where are we heading, Leif?"
"I don't know."
"When are we coming back, Leif?"
"I don't know."
"Are we coming back at all, Leif?," the voice tinged with apprehension.
"I don't know!"
"GREAT IDEA, LET'S SET SAIL! WE ARE WITH YOU!"

Were these discoveries mere luck? Or were they a blend of audacity, naivety, and boundless curiosity?

Marcel recalls an encounter with one Norwegian coltsfoot in the early 2000s—John Carew—who shared stories about playing with the legendary Italian star, Francesco Totti. Carew described Totti's simple approach to the game: "just kick the ball." There was no overthinking, no second-guessing; it was a pure, unadulterated focus on getting the ball into the goal.

Suddenly, Marcel is transported back to a defining game in his own career: the Norwegian Championship (NM) final of 2002 in Oslo. Everything came down to *one* play. The coach outlined one of their core strategies, calling Marcel as one of two options for the final shot. The stakes couldn't be higher: it was the difference between victory and defeat, between making history and being forgotten.

The inbound pass went to Ståle Skaggestad, a colleague of Marcel's in the national team. Marcel and yet another teammate were set to come off some screens. Ståle's task was clear-cut: Look for option number 1, and if he's not open, then option number 2. Nothing else.

Yet, in a surprising turn, Ståle seized the moment, posted up, and launched a perfectly arched mid-range jumper. The unmistakable "swoosh" left the audience in awe; the championship was theirs. After the game, Marcel recalled Ståle's candid admission: "All of a sudden, I wasn't sure what to do. I had the ball, I was unguarded, so I just shot."

Such pure naivety, without being bogged down by potential consequences, can be advantageous. Over the years, Marcel has often pondered this theme, trying to discern what lies behind success. He questions the external and internal factors, and given the right set of values, what makes individuals truly shine. He even finds himself reflecting on Erling Haaland's seemingly boundless self-confidence. He wonders if it's solely built on self-trust or if there's an inherent naivety in Haaland's approach: "I see the ball, I shoot, I score."

Climate Change Meets the Viking Code

Marcel and I complement each other like a healthy pairing of milk and cookies. Our shared determination propels us to go beyond the surface understanding of high performance. Our quest is profound: we seek better explanations rather than attributing it to mere naivety or serendipity. We aim to decode the essence of Norwegian excellence. We're eager to unravel the Viking Code.

Two questions particularly pique our curiosity:

- First, how do today's modern Vikings differentiate from their legendary predecessors? Put differently, why this surge of success now? How did Norwegian athletes in a much broader context transcend their nation's winter sports legacy to achieve contemporary excellence?

- Second, what enduring legacies have these modern Vikings inherited from their ancestors? Is there a latent cultural pulse, a residue of exploration and resilience, awaiting its moment to shine?

Our discussions inevitably circle back to core values—Norway's rich cultural heritage and the intriguing Law of Jante, discussed in Chapter 1.

Is the simple answer to Norwegian success transcending this communal mindset? In tandem with early talent nurturing, have individuals now been given the freedom to distinguish themselves while still thriving collectively?

While this definitely seems like a straightforward explanation, there must be more to it than a stoic pop-philosophical Seneca "meme-type" of way—"Luck is what happens when preparation meets opportunity."

Maybe there is an even more straightforward factor behind the meteoric rise of modern Norwegian athletes. Could it, quite simply, be the climate?

Every Easter holiday, Norway witnesses a migration of its back-packing and the crispy chocolate "Kvikk Lunsj"–eating populace, every one of them eager for a mountain retreat.

Back to the mountains: though winter's embrace is still felt in these elevated terrains, there's an unmistakable shift. The "snow borderline"—the altitude where snow reliably falls—is ascending. While the difference isn't alarming to most, especially with regions like Finnmark in the far north still enjoying abundant snowfall, the trend, in line with global climate change projections, is concerning. Contrast this with the Swiss or Austrian Alps, where once-thriving ski resorts now sport patches of artificial snow amid green fields, offering an almost surreal view. Norwegians, cozily watching skiing events from their homes, might ponder the longevity of these resorts.

As snow becomes a rarer sight in urban areas, Norwegians have been spurred to explore alternative activities. Given this changing landscape, one can't help but wonder: If Marit Bjørgen, hailing from central Norway, were a child today, would she still be drawn to skiing?

Interestingly, the modern Vikings making headlines in typically non-Norwegian disciplines hail from snow-free coastal regions, marked by rainy and windy winters: Casper Ruud and Victor Hovland from Oslo, Martin Ødegaard from Drammen, Erling Haaland from Bryne, the Ingebrigtsen brothers from Sandnes, and Karsten Warholm from Ulsteinvik. These locations are all strung along the coast at sea level. Even Anders Mol, from the coastal island of Stord, and Christian Sørum from Rælingen—the world's leading beach volleyball players—come from similarly snow-free environments. Sørum, the only "misfit" deemed a "bondeknøl" (or country boy), is from the Norwegian countryside, just 21.2 kilometers from the Oslo coast.

In contrast, renowned skiers like Marit Bjørgen, Petter Northug, and Ole Einar Bjørndalen are from smaller locales with easy access to snow, their aspirations molded by skier role models from previous generations.

Marcel feels it is time to get down to the hard facts.

"You are responsible for your life and your success," he declares with conviction. His urge to return to a methodical approach feels almost palpable, compelling one to "Get up and act!" With a gentle balance between nurturing and assertiveness, Marcel conveys an earnest sentiment: "While external factors may dictate the starting conditions, your reaction is entirely in your hands. You may not always control the game, but you certainly control your response to both life and the game itself."

It's My Life: Taking the Reins

"Victory awaits him who has everything in order; luck some people call it. Defeat is certain for him who has neglected to take necessary precautions in time; this is called bad luck."

—Roald Amundsen

In the stark and unpredictable terrains of both nature and sport, the difference between success and failure often lies not in blind luck, but in meticulous preparation. In *Great by Choice*, Jim Collins takes a closer look at this very principle. Collins unravels the distinguishing factors that separate wildly successful teams from the less successful ones in environments characterized by change, chaos, and uncertainty. The book doesn't just celebrate serendipity; it emphasizes the importance of disciplined preparation, methodical action, and calculated risk. Collins opens Chapter 2 of his book with the quote by Roald Amundsen showing how Amundsen's expedition to the South Pole serves as a testament to this belief. While his team reached the pole successfully, having prepared diligently for every eventuality, the British team led by Robert Falcon Scott met a tragic fate. Scott led the British Terra Nova Expedition to the Antarctic, aiming to be the first to reach the South Pole. They reached the pole on January 17, 1912, only to find that the Norwegian expedition led by Roald Amundsen had preceded them by 34 days.

On their return journey, facing exceptionally harsh weather, difficult terrain, and dwindling supplies, all five members of Scott's polar party perished. The contrast in outcomes underscores the profound impact of preparation, planning, and decision-making.

Marcel identifies a recurring trait in all the high-performers he has worked with: their unwavering ownership of their actions. These top athletes recognize that they dictate their decisions, actions, and reactions. Instead of pointing fingers at external factors when faced with setbacks, they introspectively analyze what they could have done differently. Such athletes not only set the bar high with their actions but also guide their teams by example. This attitude remains consistent, even in the face of failures or mistakes. These high-performers readily accept accountability, never hesitating to take responsibility. Over the years, this dedication to excellence, continuous learning, and understanding the ramifications of one's actions has been proven to not only elevate individual performance but also propel entire teams to greatness. What's more, this value framework isn't imposed upon them; they uphold these standards because they genuinely believe it's the righteous path.

Now deeply engrossed in his narrative, Marcel is poised to share the pillars of exceptional progress and achievement. "I wanted to bring up another point," he begins. As he continues, I come to grasp the intricate nature of our discussion, especially as we delve into what fuels the "drive" and the perpetual growth of these athletes and the source of their motivation.

In his 2009 *New York Times* bestseller, *Drive: The Surprising Truth About What Motivates Us*, Daniel H. Pink delves into human motivation, challenging traditional ideas. He suggests that autonomy, mastery, and purpose are the primary factors driving high performance and satisfaction, as opposed to the conventional reward/punishment model.

Pink posits that while extrinsic rewards, such as money, can be effective for tasks demanding straightforward, mechanical skills, they can be less effective—and even counterproductive—for tasks that necessitate conceptual, creative thinking. In these scenarios, intrinsic motivation, driven by autonomy, mastery, and purpose, proves more efficacious.

Drawing from diverse studies in psychology, economics, and business, *Drive* presents a compelling argument, offering insights and guidelines for individuals and teams eager to tap into more robust motivational strategies.

Reflecting on Marcel's words, I'm reminded of Pink's theories: "I want to bring up the point that, undoubtedly, money and gold medals are motivating factors. However, extrinsic motivation has its limits. While 'carrots' are essential, 'sticks' have their place too." Although Marcel's remarks echo Pink's sentiments, it's clear Marcel's perspective is grounded in his personal experiences on the training field. He is quick to add, "With athletes, sometimes I must push through obstacles. I'm not advocating for punishment, but rather suggesting a gentle prod to kindle a more profound, intrinsic motivation and light the fire within"

World-class achievements aren't solely defined by skill or talent. Rather, it hinges on the tenacity to hold oneself accountable, the determination to shape one's destiny, and the resilience to resist the lure of victimhood. Marcel underscores that at the heart of athletic success is this unwavering commitment to personal responsibility.

Drawing parallels with Amundsen, Marcel illuminates how elite performers are not just products but also architects of their environment. Consider Karsten Warholm and his local club, Dimna IL, in Ulsteinvik. Despite facing numerous obstacles like inclement weather, lack of equipment, and limited coaching resources, he chose not to yield. Rather than being ensnared in a narrative of external blame, he saw every challenge as a lesson, reshaping his approach after every stumble.

Just as Karsten aspired not only to reach the zenith but to redefine it, extreme personal responsibility becomes imperative. By owning every decision and perfecting every move, one can witness transcendent outcomes.

An Extraordinary Body and a Stubborn Head

Norwegians are explorers.

And I say this not merely out of national pride; throughout history, my compatriots have demonstrated an innate curiosity and adventurous spirit. Names like Roald Amundsen, Fridtjof Nansen, and Thor Heyerdahl have all reached global recognition, underlining the Norwegian spirit.

There seems to be something culturally and historically anchored in this explorative spirit. In 1896, two daring Norwegian-Americans, Captain George Harbo and first mate Frank Samuelson, set out from New York in their 18-foot wooden boat, *Fox*. Their lofty ambition? To row across the Atlantic.

This audacious idea, born one evening in a New York bar, would become a 4,000–nautical mile journey that spanned 55 days. Without the aid of modern navigation, they traversed the treacherous waters, making landfall off the coast of Cornwall before eventually docking in Le Havre, France. They were driven by a casual barroom conversation and the promise of gold medals from a magazine editor. And their feat remains unparalleled and timeless.

To underscore the gravity of this achievement, picture the year 1896. An 18-foot open wooden boat. An idea conceived during a casual night out. The objective: to ROW from New York to France. Fifty-five days later, mission accomplished.

Marcel is about to head in the opposite direction. He's boarding a plane bound for New York to meet Casper and his father, Christian, for final preparations ahead of the 143rd edition of the US Open. Over the past few years, having spent half the year on the road with Casper, Marcel has tried to limit his on-site involvement to major tournaments. Now, however, his presence is imperative.

Having reached two grand slam finals, Casper soared to the top. But recent minor injuries and tournament losses have placed him in a precarious position. Last year, he made it to the US Open final, and a poor performance this year could mean not only losing the ranking points he accrued from that run but also the risk of not qualifying for the subsequent ATP Tournament in

Torino. There, he had previously secured valuable ranking points with a semi-finals appearance.

The world ranking in tennis is determined by the points a player earns in tournaments, which are then carried over to the following year. Casper, having recently slipped a few spots, now sits at seventh as Marcel prepares to depart. An early exit from the final Grand Slam of the year (complementing the Australian Open, French Open, and Wimbledon) could result in a further slide down the rankings, perhaps by another 10 places. If he doesn't qualify to play in Torino, he could plummet to somewhere between the 20th and 30th positions. In that range, players grapple not only with up-and-coming stars on the court but also off the court, vying for headlines and sponsorship deals. Marcel's mission is crystal clear: *bring Casper to peak form in every aspect—physically and mentally.*

As Marcel packs for the hard courts of the Big Apple, we catch up digitally. While he might not be pegged for chief technology officer of the next Silicon Valley start-up—given his occasional challenges with camera settings and connectivity— once our session starts, he's all business. He's reflected on the notes I shared earlier and is keen to delve into our discussion.

I've just woken up to the news of Viktor Hovland pushing boundaries in golf once again, winning one of his most significant titles to date—the BMW Championship. Coming off a stellar 61-round close and delivering one of the best second halves ever witnessed at this level—with seven birdies in the last nine holes—Viktor demonstrated both mental and physical skills. Reflecting on his performance, he noted, "Instead of thinking that I could win, I was more focused on what was the best choice right then and there—and went for it. There were obviously some good shots, and I tried to make the best decision for every single shot." Meanwhile, Jakob Ingebrigtsen and rising star Narve

Gilje Nordås have both stormed into the 1500m final in the ongoing World Championship in athletics. The narrative of Norwegian excellence continues.

"Kristian Blummenfelt. He's a tough nut to crack, stubborn as they come," Marcel begins, leading our session with another coastal example to prove a point about the mental and physical toughness needed to make it to the top. It's as if he intuits my interest in what creates unique physical power coupled with resolute mental tenacity. Instead of a broad generalization on my part, we're zeroing in on specifics. This Bergen-born sensation, also a social media influencer, is unfamiliar to me—even with my above-average passion for sports. Yet, he's precisely where Marcel wants to start.

Kristian is a Red Bull Triathlete, making history as the first person to clinch both the Olympic gold medal and the Ironman World Championship in a single year.

It's somewhat embarrassing for me to realize that Norway not only boasts the world's top triathlete in Kristian, but also the second-best in his roommate, Gustav Ideen. And all this time, I remained unaware. Together with their coach, Olav Bu, they form what the Swiss NZZ has labeled the "most famous men's flatshare in the world."

Both are Ironman Gold and Silver medalists, aiming to replicate their achievements at the upcoming Olympics.

While mental resilience and exceptional physical prowess play a central role in their success—enabling them to challenge their own limits without the typical mental entanglements seen in other sports—Marcel's insights and research on their accomplishments shed light on the makings of an elite athlete. Yet, as our discussion progresses, I find myself increasingly captivated by another figure in their lives—their other roommate. This curious aspect further emphasizes the unique nature of the Viking Code.

"I Will Be Your Father Figure; Put Your Tiny Hand in Mine"

Kristian Blummenfelt, Gustav Iden, and their coach, leaving family behind, exemplify individuals who prioritize success above all else. Even the presence on social media is not spontaneous but a calculated facet of their broader strategy. Every detail, from shoes to equipment, is driven by data. Pleasures and parties are notably absent in their lives, replaced by an unwavering commitment to excellence and a foundation of discipline.

When probed about potential compromises, there's no limit to what they'd sacrifice. Olav Bu, their coach, often cites studies during interviews, noting, "It's proven that top athletes who enter relationships often experience a decline in performance."

A closer look at these athletes' personal lives reveals their sacrifices. Relationships evolve slowly; it's often years before they publicly acknowledge a partner or consider cohabitation. During the demanding pre-season, training sessions, and extended travel periods, these young men often find themselves in isolated training camps. Their routine becomes monotonous: eat, sleep, train, repeat—for weeks, even months on end. Thus, their journey to excellence is defined not just by what they undertake, but also by what they consciously avoid.

Ever since diving deep into the Viking Code, I've been eager to discuss these observations with Marcel.

In many cultures, mothers play pivotal roles in guiding their children's ambitions. But in Norway, it's not uncommon for fathers—or even grandfathers—to set aside their dreams and careers for their sons. Often, these men hope their children will surpass their own accomplishments.

Consider the case of Johannes Høsflot Klæbo. Destined to reshape the record books as the most successful cross-country skier, much of his success can be attributed to his grandfather,

Kåre Høsflot. Though an octogenarian, Kåre was not just a role model but also Johannes's trainer, and he is credited for the young skier's meteoric rise.

Similarly, soccer players Martin Ødegaard and Erling Haaland owe much of their success to their fathers, Hans-Erik and Alf-Inge, respectively. Both fathers abandoned early retirements and their own pursuits to cultivate their sons' talents. Christian Ruud, once ranked 39th in tennis, spurred his son Casper to reach an impressive third place ranking and amass more than US$15 million in prize money by the age of 24.

It's not always about prior expertise. Fathers become their children's most trusted allies and confidants, even with little coaching background. For instance, Henrik Carlsen took on multiple roles for his son, chess prodigy Magnus Carlsen. Gert Ingebrigtsen, despite a tumultuous relationship with his sons, has coached Henrik, Filip, and the extraordinarily gifted Jakob to numerous achievements.

Viktor Hovland's introduction to golf came from his father, Harald, who learned the game in the United States. Karsten Warholm's "replacement father" and coach—Leif Olav Alnes—is a fixture in his life, guiding him as both his siblings and father had done before.

This dynamic hearkens back to ancient Viking tales where sons often joined their fathers in ventures, eventually surpassing the older generation's achievements. These fathers, in turn, were always willing to make sacrifices for their sons' successes.

In Norway, one distinct strength is the nurturing of role models. While elite academies and fierce competitions undeniably offer statistical advantages, Marcel suggests that the success of the current generation of Vikings doesn't necessarily stem from an early specialization or elite training.

Marcel offers an insightful comparison to Brazil's favelas, or shantytowns. He suggests that while the Brazilian approach nurtures creative genius on the soccer pitch, this talent is a product of innumerable hours of practice and play. Given Brazil's large population, it's inevitable that a few extraordinary talents rise to the top, even as many potential late bloomers might be overlooked. By contrast, while Brazil's favelas house more than 12 million people, Oslo's "rougher" areas—which might seem relatively safe in a global context—have a population of just 12,000. During the 1980s and 1990s, neighborhoods on the eastern side of Oslo became notable for producing talent, with basketball players emerging from Holmlia and local athletes from diverse areas like Furuset and Vestli. However, the disparities in population, selection criteria, and upbringing between Norway's suburbs and Brazil's favelas are pronounced.

Marcel also cautions against over-reliance on elite academies. He believes it's risky for Norway to simply adopt models from more populous regions. For instance, while Rio de Janeiro's metropolitan area houses 15 million people and São Paulo boasts a population of more than 22 million, Norway's demographics are starkly different. The saying, "If you can make it in New York—or in this case in the metropolitan regions of Brazil—you can make it anywhere," perhaps resonates differently in a Norwegian context.

The Viking Code emphasizes a unique approach, different from structured elite academies. With many of these athletes now in their mid-20s, Marcel stresses the importance of recognizing the journey they've undertaken.

In the Norwegian context, paternal figures and societal role models offer a deeper understanding of an individual beyond a mere survival-of-the-fittest mentality. This intimate connection can reveal how best to nurture and develop potential. Furthermore, these role models create an environment where aspiring athletes can envision success, breaking barriers for themselves and inspiring others in the process.

The Norwegian model, encapsulated by the Viking Code, attributes its success to the foundational security it provides. This approach diverges from the typical childhood success models. It emphasizes the idea that one's potential is not capped but can be continually expanded. Instead of contending daily for mere survival, young athletes in Norway are nurtured to embrace challenges and set lofty aspirations. Historically, the Norwegian approach resembled the quiet individual who observes from the sidelines until mastering their craft. Hard work and achievement are fundamental, but there's always room for growth. This foundational safety, combined with cultural evolution, has fostered a distinct narrative for Norwegian athletes: one can excel locally—in the village, nationally, and then globally—from home to the world stage.

The self-determination theory (SDT), formulated by psychologists Edward Deci and Richard Ryan, provides an encompassing view on human motivation. Fundamentally, SDT suggests that humans have inherent psychological needs—namely competence, autonomy, and relatedness. When these needs are satisfied, individuals don't merely feel motivated; they flourish. It's among the most referenced theories in psychology. Competence pertains to the drive for mastery; autonomy underscores the need for control over actions; and relatedness stresses the value of interpersonal connections.

In elite performance circles, SDT's significance is paramount. Creating an environment where people experience competence, autonomy, and connection can catalyze heightened motivation, leading to unparalleled performance. Athletes, for example, thrive when they possess sport mastery (competence), influence their training (autonomy), and connect deeply with their teams (relatedness).

Modern Vikings seem to have inadvertently concocted a formula that, combined with current external factors, paves the way for unprecedented accomplishments.

Success is elusive. One can't help but wonder how many structured systems have overlooked talented individuals, and conversely, how many dreams have gone unrealized due to unstructured methods and a dearth of serendipity.

What stands out to me is that success transcends mere talent. Success is intentional—it requires deliberate effort. *It is voluntary, and you must will it.* As it was a thousand years ago, prosperity, progress, and success demand commitment. This Viking mentality might be deeply embedded in the DNA, informed by history and recently revitalized in broader dimensions. Interestingly, while there's inherent satisfaction in unlocking this inner zeal, there's also the underlying question: *does exerting this effort contribute to a fulfilling life?*

While today's Viking embraces BHAGs—Big Hairy Achievable Goals—it's evident there's more to the Viking Code than just core motivational tenets and extreme commitment. Another aspect influences performance where the Viking Code truly comes to life.

As Marcel concludes our online conversation, preparing to exit his car for the airport, he remarks, "Anders, your "Micro Ambition" concept intrigued me. We should delve deeper into the routines, habits, and daily endeavors that define the journey next time we meet.

Casper Ruud: Never Throw a Racket

It was with a touch of nostalgia that the Norwegian newspaper *Aftenposten* followed young Casper to his childhood home, where they shared a seemingly ordinary meal of "Brødskiver med Leverpostei." This phrase, when stripped of its cultural warmth and translated into English, becomes a rather sterile "Slice of bread with liver pâté." It's intriguing how language has this ability. What's so intimately familiar in one culture can appear strikingly alien in another, like typical breakfast scenes across Norway: families opening a yellow aluminum can, the innocent gaze of a child's face printed on it, to spread liver pâté on their morning bread. It's as quintessentially Norwegian as the Brunost, their famed brown cheese, and the beloved tradition of "Matpakke"— the simple act of wrapping slices of bread in foil, a lunchtime ritual before heading to school or work. Before diving deeper into the exact Norwegian culture, I had a rather narrow viewpoint, perceiving these traditions as the core of our identity. However, within the confines of an ordinary Norwegian home, during an interview that was anything but ordinary, a young man spoke, not of liver pâté or cheese, but of tennis, dreams, and the future.

At first glance, Casper Ruud might appear as any other tennis player with big dreams. However, there's a unique aspiration he holds onto tightly: never to let frustration get the best of him, never to throw his racket away in anger. *Aftenposten* doesn't paint Casper as a mere athlete but as a human being. It's easy to think of his achievements as outcomes of raw talent. But in truth, every move he makes, every stroke he delivers, is a direct result of the choices he makes off the court.

Christian Ruud, Casper's father, once stood at number 39 on the ATP Ranking. It was 1995, and the world of tennis looked quite different. But Christian's legacy wasn't just about ranking. It was about imparting a particular mindset to his son. Today, under his father's guidance, Casper has not only played back-to-back at Roland Garros—the French Open—and reached a US Open final but has also secured a spot among the top three tennis players worldwide.

While the arc of Casper's career might read like a fairy tale, it's underpinned by an unyielding dedication. Every day, he commits himself to a micro-ambitious minutiae of the game—something we'll explore in the next chapter. He believes in the power of compound interest in skills: small, consistent improvements that aggregate over time. At 183 centimeters and 77 kilograms, with a face reminiscent of a pop band poster boy, it's not his sheer physical power that sets him apart. He isn't the tallest or the most muscular on the court. Instead, it's his nuanced understanding of the sport, the way he approaches tennis, that has carved out his path to success.

Such a statement might seem overly simplistic, but it embodies Casper's essence. While some might argue that he lacks the raw edges required to dominate the game entirely, his success tells a different story. His nimble footwork, solid tennis fundamentals, and remarkable mental fortitude have crafted his winning formula. But what truly distinguishes him on the tour isn't just his technical acumen. It's his sheer love for the game and the respect he showers upon everyone around him, making Casper Ruud an invaluable asset to modern tennis.

Casper was a head starter. His journey with tennis began seemingly the moment he entered this world. There's a particular photo in the family album that's often revisited: a toddler-aged Casper, dragging a bucket filled to the brim with tennis balls, almost as tall as he was. But these early encounters with the sport were more about a child's curiosity than a deep-seated passion. It was only around the age of 10 or 11 that Casper vocalized a genuine interest in playing tennis. Yet, even as he entered his early teens, his commitment to the court remained sporadic.

One of Casper's most vivid memories from childhood was watching Rafael Nadal—a prodigious 19-year-old—lift his first French Open trophy. It was a moment in history, as Nadal became the first player since Mats Wilander in 1982 to clinch the title on his debut. That day, a six-year-old Casper watched with wide eyes, perhaps unaware of the foreshadowing of his own destiny. Fast-forward to June 5, 2022: the clay courts of Roland Garros would bear witness to a remarkable full-circle moment. Casper Ruud, having clawed his way to the final, would face off against none other than Rafael Nadal, now a seasoned 36-year-old veteran. Adding a touch of serendipity to the occasion, the commentator in the stadium that day was Mats Wilander. The narrative seemed perfectly set for a symbolic passing of the torch. Yet reality had other plans. Facing his childhood idol, perhaps the weight of the moment bore down on Casper. The match ended with Nadal triumphant in three straight sets.

But this wasn't just a story of fan meeting idol. Casper, with his father Christian guiding him, had been molded and mentored at the Rafael Nadal Academy. Located in Nadal's hometown Manacor, on the island of Mallorca, Spain, the academy not only focuses on tennis training but also emphasizes education and personal development for its students. When he first arrived there, he was ranked 143rd in the world, with eyes set on breaking into the top 100. Under the tutelage of the academy and with Christian's watchful supervision, Casper soon adopted strategies and techniques that would see his ranking skyrocket to 24th. Their combined expertise culminated in a coaching and game plan that showed its mettle against even the fiercest of opponents. For example, during the US Open semi-final, Ruud's choice to stand far behind the baseline while returning serves was strategic, an attempt to dominate rallies right from the baseline. His impeccable footwork, his ability to transition from defense to attack, and his knack for delivering deep groundstrokes, became his signature moves. All these skills were on full display in a marathon 55-shot rally that would eventually pave his way to the US Open final.

Having had the chance to play for the ultimate dream—the number one spot—Casper Ruud still might have his best days ahead of him. Yet, what truly distinguishes Casper isn't just his success on the court, but an almost paradoxical quality: his extraordinariness lies in his ordinariness. It's reminiscent of that slice of bread with liver pâté—a staple, something so typical and perhaps even mundane. But within the framework of a culture that celebrates the ordinary, it's this very ordinariness that births something unparalleled.

Norway, a nation not necessarily synonymous with tennis legends, has given us Casper Ruud. And while his strokes, serves, and smashes echo world-class skill, it's his unwavering dedication to the nuances—the "small wins" of the game—that crafts the larger, more awe-inspiring image of his career. He doesn't merely play the game; he chooses to weave in the values that define him as an individual. In Casper Ruud, we witness a compelling testament to the harmonious blend of deep-rooted values and peak performance. He's a modern Viking showing that true progress and the success it brings are acts of will—voluntary and driven by your own determination.

4

Micro-ambitions

I RECALL ONE of the earliest insights Marcel shared with me: "In the simplicity of focusing on the task lies the essence of true wonder."

I catch up with Marcel amid the final preparations for the US Open. "I've only got 20–30 minutes today, Anders," he says with a sense of urgency. I can feel the concentration, the meticulous breaking down of days, hours, and even minutes into digestible chunks of work.

While the spotlight often shines on grand achievements, it's the smaller, day-to-day objectives that truly pave the way to success. These "micro-ambitions" represent the careful and strategic planning behind the making of a champion. It's these micro- ambitions that propel one forward amid fatigue. They provide a solid foundation and assurance when the pressure mounts.

I am deeply convinced that life operates on the principle of "compound interest." Whether it's happiness, health, wealth, family, relationships, or any other domain, the accumulated value from our efforts acts as a cushion during challenging times. Darren Hardy, in his 2012 *New York Times* bestseller,

The Compound Effect, elucidates how decisions, no matter how small, ultimately shape our destiny. "No gimmicks. No hyperbole. No magic bullet," Hardy says, emphasizing that it's the daily choices we make that determine whether we approach the life we desire or unknowingly veer toward disaster.

When discussing micro-ambitions in the context of high-performance athletes, it implies a focus on small, attainable goals that, when aggregated, culminate in significant achievements. Instead of solely focusing on a broad ambition (like clinching a gold medal or setting a world record), an athlete zeroes in on numerous smaller targets, each realistic yet progressively challenging.

Another illuminating read on the subject is James Clear's *Atomic Habits: An Easy & Proven Way to Build Good Habits & Break Bad Ones.* Embracing a micro-ambitious approach means narrowing our focus to the minutiae of progress, enabling us to break free from detrimental habits. Clear masterfully conveys the potency of habits, using the analogy of atoms. Just as atoms bond to form more substantial structures, atomic habits come together to produce noticeable results. In essence, Clear, through a broader lens, encapsulates the essential attributes of becoming a high-performance athlete:

- **Make habits obvious:** Design cues and reminders that trigger the habit consistently.
- **Make habits attractive:** Associate some satisfaction or reward with the habit to make it appealing.
- **Make habits easy:** Reduce friction and simplify the habit as much as possible.
- **Make habits satisfying:** Ensure the habit delivers intrinsic satisfaction and joy.
- **Gradually build habits:** Start very small, increase bit by bit until the habit sticks.

- **Create a habit scorecard:** Quantify habits to monitor progress.
- **Go for 1% improvements:** Small gains compound into big results.
- **Address the source of habits:** Focus on changing identity and beliefs, not just outcomes.

Atomic Habits emphasizes the importance of starting small, tracking progress, and maintaining consistency over time to achieve goals.

What I describe as being "micro-ambitious" fundamentally represents the pursuit of continuous, incremental progress—*positive and infinite progress*—which ultimately culminates in breakthrough moments or extraordinary achievements.

"Can we do a quick exercise today?" I ask Marcel.

From his expression, I can tell he's pondering how I intend to introduce a new topic amid his already packed schedule. He'd been prepared to offer succinct feedback on some reflections I'd previously shared. Currently, he's engrossed in the final preparations for what could be the most crucial event in Casper Ruud's career so far, where attention to every detail is imperative.

"*I'd like to conduct a 'lightning round' with you,*" I explain. "I'm aiming to capture your top 10 takeaways—actionable insights that anyone can start implementing immediately."

Marcel appears slightly taken aback. Nevertheless, I believe this is the opportune moment to put the man responsible for Casper's stringent physical regimen in the spotlight. Both Marcel and Casper have heavily relied on objective metrics to train effectively and to maintain the right intensity. Beyond data analysis—a step many often misinterpret—the subjective experience is equally valuable. Marcel possesses a comprehensive playbook and a wealth of insights. Now, I'm eager to distill the core principles guiding the daily journey toward mastery.

"I always believe it's important to define the larger vision," he begins. Instantly, my memory of the late Dr. Stephen R. Covey springs to life. I recall our meeting back in 2012 during his last visit to Europe. Tragically, he never recovered from a bicycle accident later that year. During our encounter, we spent an hour discussing his iconic *7 Habits of Highly Effective People*. Covey, gripping his Indian talking-stick in one hand and holding my hand in the other—which felt like an eternity—left a profound mark on me, particularly with Habit 2: "Begin with the End in Mind." Covey described this habit as the power to envision what is not yet visible to the eye. He believed all things come into existence twice: first mentally and then physically. The tangible realization mirrors its mental conception, much like a building arises from a blueprint. Without a conscious effort to visualize our aspirations and who we wish to become, we inadvertently allow others and external circumstances to shape our destiny. It emphasizes reconnecting with one's uniqueness and setting personal, moral, and ethical boundaries within which one can thrive.

Marcel, now squarely in the spotlight, is prepared and eager to delve in.

"Next, it's essential to break down the main goal," he continues. "With my athletes, I deconstruct the primary objective into smaller, more achievable tasks or milestones. For instance, when someone is on the recovery path from an injury, we segment the recovery journey into weekly progress goals."

Furthermore, it's vital to establish daily tasks. Be it training, adhering to sleep schedules, maintaining proper nutrition, or managing obligations outside the sport, I emphasize the importance of translating milestones into daily or weekly tasks.

"Is this point number four?" Marcel queries. "Prioritize consistency. It's about committing to show up on time every day, especially when the journey feels painstakingly slow. Over time, consistency yields compounding benefits."

Celebrate small wins. Marcel staunchly believes in setting aside moments to acknowledge and celebrate the achievement of micro-ambitions. It not only sustains motivation but also fortifies positive behavior.

Monitoring progress is equally significant. Utilize technology when feasible. Whether through a journal or a digital tool, maintaining a record of daily tasks and advancements is pivotal. Visual representations of consistency and milestones achieved can be a powerful source of motivation.

"In today's fast-evolving world, adaptability is paramount," Marcel emphasizes. While maintaining consistency is indispensable, being prepared to adjust strategies on the fly is equally critical. "If an approach doesn't yield the desired results, we should be ready to learn and pivot." The unpredictability of how sports will evolve in the next 5 to 10 years underscores this sentiment. "And, to this point," Marcel adds, "I'd emphasize 'Stay Educated.' The world, along with techniques, is in a rapid state of flux. It's imperative to stay abreast with the latest knowledge and tactics pertinent to our goals.

"I think this next point naturally follows the last: **Seek Feedback.** We can't achieve greatness in isolation. Regular consultations with mentors, coaches, or peers is a necessity. **Collaboration is key.** If feasible, partner with someone or a group who shares similar goals. Such collaborations not only boost motivation and ensure accountability but also bring in fresh perspectives. Surrounding oneself with experts in various fields, especially those superior in certain skills, can provide invaluable insights to refine your micro-ambitions and ensure you're on the right track.

"For the ninth point, I'd emphasize **Limit Distractions,** Marcel continues. "In our fast-paced, multitasking world, zeroing in on a single task can be quite a feat. It's imperative to create an environment that fosters concentration. This might mean disabling notifications, designating specific work hours, or simply seeking a tranquil workspace. As athletes garner more attention for their feats, distractions amplify. Hence, mastering the art of eliminating interruptions should be ingrained from the very beginning.

Tenth on my list would be Mindset. Nurturing a growth mindset and staying anchored to your core reasons or 'why' is paramount. Have unwavering faith in your potential to evolve and better yourself. During challenging phases, it helps to revisit the reasons that spurred your journey. Such intrinsic motivation propels you past hurdles, keeping you resolute in your micro-ambitions. Always remember: each obstacle or setback paves the way for learning, and progress is perpetually within reach.

"May I add one more?" Marcel inquires.

"Of course," I respond.

"Plan for Rest, Reflection, and Refinement," he offers. "I've told you before: training breaks you down, but it's rest that facilitates growth. Additionally, it's essential to occasionally take a breather, evaluate your strides, and determine if your micro-ambitions are inching you closer to your overarching goal. If they aren't, recalibrate and march forward."

To Do or Not to Do

Incorporating micro-ambitions into your personal strategy can be transformative. It's not just about the end goal but valuing each step along the journey. Recognizing that every incremental achievement contributes to the larger objective allows for focused progress. Discussing micro-ambitions, thus, emphasizes a detail-oriented approach.

The benefits of adopting a micro-ambitions strategy are clear. Done right, this is where momentum is built. Regularly achieving these smaller goals offers continual boosts of confidence and motivation. Each accomplished micro-ambition provides a sense of achievement, further propelling you forward.

Micro-ambitions lie at the heart of the Viking Code and are something Norwegian athletes have emphasized for decades. Norwegians are often described as rational and pragmatic. In sports, Norwegian soccer players are treasured assets on any team because they're straightforward and reliable: they "get the job done." With no fuss or drama, they consistently show up for training on time and stick to the plan.

A prime illustration of this is the Ingebrigtsen brothers—Jakob, Henrik, and Filip. The Norwegian running family entered the scene when athletes from Africa dominated the middle distances, while Europeans were nowhere to be seen. The brothers have achieved their remarkable results, largely due to the rigorous daily regimen devised by their father, Gjert. When the brothers parted ways with him, Gjert, within a year, sculpted another athlete—Narve Gilje Nordås—into world-class form. Gjert Ingebrigtsen with no coaching background—has even stated he is not interested in sport—regards each training session, run, and diet plan as a "micro-ambition." Instead of merely aiming to win races, he underscores the importance of daily discipline, consistency, and meticulous training. The brothers' success story embodies the belief that championships aren't won on race day but during the numerous unseen hours of preparation.

Similarly, Ole Einar Bjørndalen, hailed as the "king of biathlon" and the most medaled Olympian in Winter Olympic Games history, exhibited this commitment to detail during his career. Bjørndalen converted a truck into an altitude-training bedroom, simulating alpine sleeping conditions. His off-season shooting practices were decomposed into minute tasks, honing every element from posture to breathing and trigger techniques. Bjørndalen's illustrious career can be compared to a mosaic: each "micro-ambition" forms part of a grand masterpiece.

There's an analogy often cited in motivational talks about the Chinese bamboo tree. After planting its seed, you see no visible sign of growth for up to 5 years. But then, in the fifth year, the bamboo tree grows up to 80 feet in just 6 weeks. However, it's not that the bamboo tree grew 80 feet in 6 weeks; it grew 80 feet in 5 years. During those unseen years, a massive root system is spreading underground, preparing the bamboo for rapid, explosive growth. Similarly, athletes may not see immediate results, but with patience, persistence, and consistent efforts (their "micro-ambitions"), they achieve explosive success.

Be Unique

Micro-ambitions are fundamentally about clarity and refined focus. When athletes' goals are too broad, it becomes easy to overlook critical aspects of their training or performance. By adopting a micro-ambitions approach, athletes can concentrate on specific facets of their discipline, fostering mastery over time.

As Marcel prepares to leave for his next session, he pauses, sharing a keen observation. "I often notice people resorting to overgeneralizations. They lack specificity," he starts. "I believe this arises from a combination of laziness and ingrained thought patterns. You should look into a concept called 'learned helplessness' by Dr. Martin Seligman," he suggests before logging out.

Dr. Seligman links such tendencies to certain neurological pathways in the brain. He describes three Ps that are often indicative of overgeneralization:

Pervasive: Absolutes like "they," "everybody," "totally," "everyone," and "Completely" infiltrate our vocabulary. It's the kind of sweeping statement we see in claims like "They always do X," or "They never do Y." These broad generalizations often sidestep a deeper understanding of the issue at hand.

Permanent: This refers to the use of terms like "always," "never," and "every time." Such terms can be more constructively replaced with "occasionally" or "sometimes," offering a more empowering and accurate perspective, especially when compared to the frequent misuse by certain media outlets.

Personal: Phrases like "How could I be so stupid?" rarely offer constructive introspection. Taking things too personally can hinder progress and self-growth.

Being aware of these patterns enables us to communicate more effectively, sidestepping obstacles that impede understanding and advancement. Reflecting on our discussions, I recognize that this precision in communication has been a consistent theme in my talks with Marcel. This clarity, by focusing on specifics, makes insights tangible and actionable, ultimately driving progress.

As Marcel eloquently expressed, "In the simplicity of focusing on the task lies the essence of true wonder."

How Micro-ambitions Drive Success

Experiencing personal progress can be deeply fulfilling. There's a unique satisfaction in giving overarching purpose to one's life. It appears that modern-day Vikings have harnessed the art of micro-ambitions, allowing them to savor each step forward and have learned to enjoy progress. Three aspects underscore the potency of micro-ambitions:

- **Measurable Progress:** With micro-ambitions, one can continuously gauge progress. Athletes who fall short on a specific minor goal have the opportunity to tweak their strategy or technique, ensuring larger ambitions remain intact.
- **Adaptability:** Focusing on bite-sized objectives enables athletes to adapt swiftly to changing circumstances. Whether these changes are physical, shifts in competition, or external advancements in technology and training, micro-ambitions offer the agility needed.
- **Mitigating Pressure:** Large, overarching goals, while motivating, can sometimes be overwhelming, leading to performance-related stress. Segmenting these ambitions into manageable, immediate tasks helps athletes handle

pressure adeptly, centering their attention on the immediate challenge rather than the ultimate objective.

Embracing this mindset unlocks the essence of the Viking Code. Life becomes a series of playful, enjoyable tasks that simplify the journey toward success.

But this raises a chicken-or-egg quandary: Does the joy and playfulness position you to hone the foundational skills for elite performance, or is it the other way around? In essence, *which came first: the joy or the grind?*

Viktor Hovland: A Norse Life in Fortune and Fame

At the East Lake Golf Club, the atmosphere was electric. As the sun set, casting a golden hue over the course, spectators gathered around the 18th hole, eager to witness history in the making. Viktor Hovland, the boyish wonder from Oslo, stood confidently at the tee, taking in the sight of thousands of fans cheering him on. His journey from the quiet greens of Norway to the bustling courses of America had been nothing short of spectacular.

The pressure was immense. Holding a lead in the FedExCup, especially with players like Xander Schauffele breathing down your neck, is no small feat. But Hovland's composure, perfected from his years in the sport, was evident. With every swing, he displayed a finesse that came from relentless practice, commitment, and an innate passion for the game.

Each hole he conquered brought him closer to that coveted title. By the time he approached the 17th hole, he had built a significant lead, and it seemed almost certain that the trophy would be his. However, in golf, as in life, nothing is ever guaranteed until the final putt is holed.

On the 18th hole, Hovland took a moment to absorb the scene around him. The cheering crowds, the shimmering water hazards—it was the culmination of years of hard work and determination. Taking a deep breath after a brief visit to the bunker near the green, he lined up his shot. With a gentle touch, he sent the ball landing neatly on the green, setting himself up for a birdie putt to conclude the tournament. "He is the season-long victor," the commentator remarked, delighting in a play on words.

The FedExCup was his. At just 25, Viktor Hovland had clinched one of golf's most prestigious titles and established himself as a force to be reckoned with on the global stage. The weekend had been transformative, not just for Hovland, but for the world of golf. Besides the Formula 1 season-series, the FedExCup is the highest paid sport tournament to be won by any individual. With winnings of a staggering US$18 million, Hovland's mastery on the greens had him outshine Xander Schauffele by a neat five shots. Everyone else? They lagged more than 10 shots behind.

Schauffele, though defeated, was gracious. "I never had so much fun losing. I played a round of 62 but still lost by 5 shots, I can only congratulate Hovland for his great game over the past week," he commented.

The newspapers didn't waste any time. Yet in a following interview, Hovland demurred, "The money is nice for the family." He continued: "I do not need much. I do not find purpose in the prizes; there are other things that drive me." Almost as if to underscore this point, Hovland was spotted the next day. No, not in a luxury lounge or a celebrity hotspot. He was in an airport, dressed in everyday jeans, carrying a nondescript rucksack, boarding a standard flight back for a short visit to Norway.

Just a week earlier, Hovland had clinched victory at the BMW Championship. In a game dominated by players primarily from the United States and Great Britain, Hovland hailed from a country celebrated for winter sports, where golfers annually grapple with the challenge of finding real grass surfaces.

What sets Hovland apart on the tour? It's not just his skill with a club. The German commentators, known for their reserved style, can't help but gush, "Everyone loves Viktor." And it's easy to see why.

Beyond his obvious talent lies his trademark: an infectious smile, a friendly demeanor, and an innate inclination to serve others.

By early 2023, having ended a promising 2022 season, Hovland took a surprising turn. Hovland had a commendable season, but his meteoric rise was marred by a flaw: his game "around the green" ranked him at 191 on the tour. Despite such deficits, his stats painted an impressive picture. He featured in the top 25 in a staggering 18 of his 23 starts. He not only entered the playoffs at seventh but also achieved the uncommon feat of making the cut in all his starts.

But Hovland, paradoxically, took a step back, only to leap immeasurably forward. He amicably parted ways with Alan Bratton, his mentor, the very architect who sculpted him from the world's best amateur into a top-10 global contender. The same Bratton who had ushered him into Oklahoma State University on a coveted scholarship. But you see, for Hovland, the journey wasn't about accolades or positions; it was about evolution, about relentless, ceaseless progression.

He sought out Joseph Mayo, a visionary coach. Under Mayo's tutelage, fortified by intricate technical analyses, Hovland fine-tuned the minutiae of his game. The results were transformative. He skyrocketed nearly 100 positions in Strokes Gained: Around-the-Green, a ringing endorsement of his collaboration with Mayo. Marrying consistency with peak performance turned Hovland into an indomitable force, outclassing his peers by averaging 66.2 strokes per round in the FedExCup Playoffs. His last 11 rounds? All under 70. In essence, he outperformed the field average by an astounding 2.75 strokes per round.

In a quintessentially Hovland fashion, when queried during an interview about his success, he redirected the narrative. You see, while many bask in the ephemerality of victories, for Hovland, the allure lies in returning to the drawing board, immersing himself once more in the art of refinement. At the core of Viktor Hovland's ethos is an insatiable yearning for progress, a pursuit he lovingly refers to as his paramount passion. "I don't need much, I like routines," a statement symbolic for his approach to the game.

In an age of overwhelming choices, where success often opens floodgates of distractions, Hovland seems to have cracked a code. By intentionally streamlining his off-the-field decisions, he effectively sidesteps the snare of "decision fatigue." For an athlete of his stature, who's now in a position to chase every endorsement under the sun, he chooses, instead, to conserve that cognitive energy. Why? So he can channel every ounce of it into those razor-sharp, pivotal decisions that define moments both in practice and during crunch situations in tournaments.

So it comes as no surprise that while many athletes make headlines for endeavors outside of their sport, Hovland's actions after the 2023 BMW Championship were quintessentially him. Instead of basking in the afterglow of his triumph, he was back on the greens the very next day. But he wasn't there to play; he was shouldering clubs, caddying for his former roommate across 36 holes, aiming to help him qualify for the US Open. Hovland was there not just to support but to learn and grow. His actions underscore a belief in collective betterment and unwavering dedication to progress. Viktor Hovland isn't merely a champion golfer; he's a champion human being. A mensch. And this chapter is just the beginning of his story.

And this meticulous method, this alchemy of continuous micro-enhancements coupled with unwavering mental tenacity, hasn't just propelled Hovland to the zenith of golf—it has made him an emblematic figure in a sport that captivates half a billion hearts worldwide.

Hovland brings self-confidence to the game. He trusts in progress. Like Warholm, Haaland, and Ruud, Hovland brings a friendly force, uniting self-confidence, playfulness, and values. Hovland remembers an encounter with the "Norwegian Queen of Golf," Suzann Pettersen, that shaped his career. You might remember her from Chapter 1. At a tender age of 13, Hovland met Pettersen, then a leading figure on the LPGA tour. He described this encounter, painting a vivid picture of what was possible at the summit of the sport. Her mere presence seemed to galvanize a generation. For Hovland, his recollections of her were distinct. In a candid conversation with the LPGA ahead of the PGA Championship in 2021, he reminisced about the sheer force of Pettersen's determination—her unwavering grit, her relentless pursuit of perfection. "She was so stubborn, I was almost scared of her," Hovland admitted.

But then there was the softer side to Pettersen, often eclipsed by her competitive zeal. Journalists often quipped that her infectious smile had the uncanny ability to "light up rooms and lift spirits." Back in 2020, Pettersen had already recognized the spark in Hovland. After witnessing his mesmerizing performance at the Mayakoba Golf Classic in Mexico, she prophetically declared, "For Viktor, the sky isn't even the limit." And the wheels of fate would turn full circle when, just months later, she'd find herself extolling Hovland's achievements, bestowing upon him the accolade for the Sports Performance of the Year for 2021, a distinction that saw him outshine even the likes of Erling Braut Haaland and Karsten Warholm. With the two generations of golf bridging the drive for perfection, together with playfulness and a great smile, lies the story of Victor Hovland. In that smile, in the legacy, and the belief in one's own strengths, lies a tale of inspiration, perseverance, and the inextricable bonds that shape champions and the collective.

5

Joyful, Joyful: From the Cultivation of Play to the Mastery of the Game

"KONGEN PÅ HAUGEN" is the game "King of the Hill" in Norway. I vividly recall the older kids protecting a massive pile of snow during our school recesses. It's a seemingly straightforward game, guided by one simple rule: *there are no rules.* Well, perhaps, except for the unwritten ethos of respect. The basic idea is that children try to stand atop a mound (or snow pile in the winter) while others attempt to push them off. It's not just about physical strength, but strategy, balance, resilience, and even alliance-building. These very skills, albeit in a more sophisticated manner, could be likened to what you observe when Norwegian skiers tactically position themselves for that final sprint in a cross-country skiing race, after enduring 49.5 kilometers (30.75 miles).

From an early age, Norwegian children are nurtured to embrace the outdoors, irrespective of weather conditions. There's a popular saying—"Det finnes ikke dårlig vær, bare dårlige klær!"—which means "There's no bad weather, only bad clothing!"—that represents a typical Norwegian household's sentiment. Whether it's snow, sleet, or rain, children are found skiing, hiking, or immersed in imaginative play amid the majestic trees and fjords. I can personally attest to how this free, unstructured play cultivates creativity, resilience, and an enduring bond with nature, from my own upbringing in Norway. Central to this way of living is the principle of "Friluftsliv," best translated as "open-air living," a term capturing Norway's profound love for nature. The individual words mean "FREE," "AIR," and "LIFE"— such a beautiful composition!

Though the rugged landscapes might seem averse to fostering a culture of play and Norwegians might be seen as conservative and somewhat up-tight, it's quite the opposite—at least when it comes to actually "play." In the land of the midnight sun and aurora borealis, play, particularly outdoor play, is of utmost cultural importance.

For Norwegians, nature isn't a place visited occasionally in a planned and structured manner; *it's a playground and an integral part of daily life.*

Now, when I visit, even in remote areas, I notice an impressive offering of playgrounds and sports facilities, sadly often deserted. Undoubtedly, even in Norway, the allure of handheld devices competes with outdoor play, impacting the very essence and psychology of childhood development. Yet, in the context of the Viking Code, invaluable wisdom is to be learned here.

The Psychology of Play

Around the globe, the sports and games children engage in during schoolyard breaks echo larger societal frameworks. They serve as lessons in teamwork, leadership, the highs of success, the lows of failure, strategic thinking, and perseverance. Historically, play has been more than just an entertaining pastime; it has functioned as a potent tool for learning and personal growth.

The delight that arises from play isn't solely an ephemeral emotion. It has deep roots in our neurochemistry. Engaging in play prompts our brain to release a blend of DOSE (dopamine, oxytocin, serotonin, and endorphin) chemicals. These neurotransmitters, colloquially termed the "feel-good" chemicals, are pivotal in our pleasure and reward circuits. They underpin our motivation, facilitate our learning, and spark our innate curiosity.

Since the dawn of our species, play has transcended mere amusement. It's been an evolutionary instrument, central to our growth and learning. While games like tag or hide-and-seek might appear trivial on the surface, they are foundational experiences that inculcate core principles of strategy, social dynamics, and even the rudiments of physics.

This penchant for play isn't exclusive to humans. Many other species, especially mammals, exhibit playful behaviors in their formative years. Lion cubs indulge in mock fights, not just for fun but to sharpen their predatory skills. Birds experiment with their vocal ranges, leading to the intricate and melodious songs that grace our ears. Dolphins partake in playful acts, from riding the waves to playfully tossing seaweed using their fins, enhancing both their agility and their social bonds.

Success in playful endeavors triggers our brains to release dopamine, fortifying the behavior and spurring us to replicate it. Over time, this positive reinforcement becomes a formidable learning mechanism. It's the chemical rationale explaining the addictive allure of games proffering rewards, even if they're virtual.

For athletes, grasping this interplay is game-changing. Weaving play into training sessions not only makes them more enjoyable but also augments motivation. This dopamine-fueled feedback mechanism ensures athletes stay engrossed, accelerate their learning, and retain acquired skills for extended periods.

Play Versus Game

What may seem straightforward is often complicated in today's metric-driven world. Many instinctively equate play with risk, as play doesn't occur in a controlled environment, and therefore, injuries can occur. Moreover, playful actions may be perceived as a lack of focus and seriousness like Gaël Monfils in tennis and Ronaldinho Gaúcho in soccer, who excited the fans and brought about special skills but were also perceived as reckless. After all, the ultimate goal is winning, where there seems to be no room for playful mistakes. This perspective is evident not only in specialized sports but also in attempts to mitigate risks by standardizing playgrounds and fitting every activity into a measurable framework. This shift is a move toward the "game."

Games have been around for millennia, marking the growth and evolution of civilizations. From ancient board games in Mesopotamia to the Olympics in Greece, structured play has always been integral to society. While free play acts as a canvas for creativity and exploration, organized sports bring their own unique advantages.

However, the term *game* should not be casually equated with *play*. A game inherently possesses structure and purpose.

An interesting philosophical take, with theological undertones, comes from theologian James P. Carse in his book *Finite and Infinite Games—A Vision of Life as Play and Possibility*. Though published in 2013, decades later, it's captivating to see Carse's insights into the significance of play and possibility, not just in high-performance sport, but in life itself.

Carse delves deep, distinguishing, as he puts it, between two main types of games (or life approaches): finite and infinite.

Finite games have a clear beginning, middle, and end. They are forms of structured play, often seen in organized sports and games, with clearly defined rules and objectives. These rules provide a framework, allowing players to experiment, strategize, and develop. By mirroring real-world challenges in a controlled setting, finite games bolster cognitive development, honing skills like strategic thinking, problem-solving, and teamwork.

The primary objective of a finite game is to win. It concludes when there is a victor. Success in such games results in victory. The rules are agreed upon and constant; if broken, the game might halt or a penalty could ensue. These games are framed by external definitions, bounded by time constraints, specific rules, or physical spaces. Participants are predetermined, and the games have established outcomes or goals.

Infinite games, on the other hand, do not have a definitive beginning or end. The primary purpose of infinite games is to keep the game in play. Infinite games are played with the aim of continuing play and bringing more players into the game. Rules can change, and they are adaptable. They evolve to prevent the game from ending and to prolong the play. These games are internally defined and have boundaries that are fluid. Players can change, and the number of players might vary. There is no set "winning" outcome. The journey and continuation are more important than any end point.

How does the philosophy of finite and infinite games relate to the Viking Code? Simply put, to truly succeed in finite games, one must deeply understand and immerse oneself in the infinite game. This strive toward dynamic balance of the two appears to be intrinsic to the Norwegian approach.

While finite games—such as Olympic events or individual matches—are where medals, fame, and fortune are won, it's the infinite pursuit of progress and new opportunities that push boundaries. This not only allows for peak performances but also elevates the baseline, setting the stage for continued growth. Infinite games encourage exploration of potential and a willingness to venture beyond established boundaries. In contrast, finite games focus on maximizing and optimizing within set parameters to achieve a specific performance.

Carse encourages readers to reflect on the types of games they engage in and the implications of these choices. He posits that adopting an infinite game mindset can deeply enrich one's experiences. It's within this philosophy that we uncover a foundational element of the Viking Code: the infusion of fun and joy into development, stepping beyond the strict confines of competition.

Marcel consistently emphasizes the importance of fostering this infinite mindset, particularly during early developmental phases in order to spark creativity and enable growth. Such an exploration of potential is paramount for athletes achieving peak performance. Putting athletes in predicaments they have to solve, with an open answer can be one way of triggering this playful behavior. It's at this intersection that the true magic of the Viking Code comes alive.

A Universal Model for Success

From the moment I met Marcel, in every conversation and session, he consistently emphasized, "Du må pirre nysgjerrigheten"— "You must stimulate curiosity."

When you tap into this innate sense of wonder and remove inhibitions and fears, simple prompts like "just throw the ball," "just run the track," or "just kick the ball" ignite motor development, setting the stage for learning. Over time, this ignites motivation, which, with continued progress, can evolve into mastery. Marcel firmly believes that all training methodologies should prioritize the significance of curiosity and playfulness, especially in the formative years.

As I write this, sprinter Karsten Warholm has just showcased his dominance in the world of athletics by securing his third world championship gold medal. On the website of the Norwegian

Sports Federation (Norges Idrettsforbund), I find an older interview with a gold-adorned Warholm titled "Kids should not specialize too early to become champions." Warholm and his coach embody the principles of diversity, creativity, and play. Warholm believes there's no definitive answer regarding when sports clubs should pivot to specialization. In Dimna sports club, which he represents, the predominant emphasis has been on encouraging play, fostering positive social learning environments, and bolstering motivation. For Warholm, this philosophy has undeniably underpinned his successes.

"At a young age, a playful approach to sports is indispensable," says Warholm. "However, it's equally crucial to commit added effort to sculpting nurturing social environments that embrace all, irrespective of their performance tier. When youngsters eagerly anticipate their training sessions, growth, outcomes, and the valor to push their boundaries follow organically."

Many examples showcase the powerful connection between play and high performance.

Consider Brazil's "Futsal Magic." This quicker, more compact version of soccer is often credited for the outstanding ball control and rapid decision-making of Brazilian soccer maestros. In Brazil's tight alleyways and sunlit beaches, Futebol da Rua, or street soccer, transcends being just a game. It's a fusion of dance, drama, and festivity. The absence of stringent soccer rules means young players exhibit an uninhibited style, often inventing rules on the spot and adapting to street irregularities. Without an official referee, teams must collaboratively resolve fouls and disputes. This environment has become a breeding ground for creativity, possibly elucidating why Brazil consistently produces soccer players of dazzling finesse.

This playful approach hasn't escaped structured training regimes either. FC Barcelona's La Masia Academy, renowned globally, has incorporated and fine-tuned it. Central to this esteemed academy's philosophy is the idea that budding players must first grasp and savor the game. Training typically commences with rondos—small-sided games where players form a circle, attempting to retain possession from those in the middle. It appears simplistic, even reminiscent of children at play, but it's instrumental in refining technical prowess, vision, and split-second decision-making. This playful training ethos significantly contributes to Barcelona's international acclaim.

The Golden State Warriors' basketball dominance also pivots around a playful foundation. Viral videos frequently spotlight their MVP, Stephen "Steph" Curry, famed as one of basketball's greatest shooters and dribblers. He's often seen nonchalantly shooting from unconventional spots during warm-ups, including from the stands. The NBA team, celebrated for its fluid gameplay and shooting expertise, accentuates keeping practices lively and entertaining. Head Coach Steve Kerr, an alumnus of the Michael Jordan era, is known to kick off sessions with spontaneous half-court shot contests and similar activities. Such an ambiance encourages creativity, granting players the liberty to experiment without dreading errors.

Play is a natural antidote to stress, curbing cortisol—the body's primary stress hormone. For elite athletes, perpetually under the spotlight and pressure, infusing elements of play can be revitalizing. It affords a fresh perspective and zest toward their discipline. Our brains are inherently inclined to revel in play. The ensuing joy, motivation, and learning can be traced back to eons of evolutionary progression. This trajectory has steered various species, humans included, toward flourishing and survival, all through the deceptively simple act of playing.

If You Stop Playing, You Risk Growing Up: The Norse Master-mix

In Norwegian, there's a lyrical saying that translates to "If you believe you have learned all there is to know, you haven't merely completed your learning, you're done." This captures the idea that an endgame mindset can signal the downfall of any endeavor.

Marcel has been tied up for several weeks. Ever since we met, I've been eager to discuss a topic with him that he has always emphasized as central to high performance. Marcel thrives on face-to-face discussions, believing personal interaction to be both his strength and preferred method of imparting knowledge. So, I was taken aback when, instead of a conversation, I received a comprehensive document from him. In it, Marcel had meticulously written down the benefits he's observed tied to the act of kindling curiosity—"pirre nyskjerrigheten"—and retaining the element of play in training and development.

Marcel staunchly believes in the strong link between an athlete's well-being and their prowess. While it might be reductive to say happier athletes always outperform their less contented counterparts, there's ample evidence indicating that positive emotional states and psychological health can indeed amplify performance, and Marcel does have science and research on his side to back this claim.

In his book *Play: How It Shapes the Brain, Opens the Imagination, and Invigorates the Soul*, Dr. Stuart Brown explores the significance and science of play. Asserting that play is an essential, innate behavior, he sheds light on how it shapes our brains, fosters creativity, and aids in problem-solving. Drawing on extensive research, the book underscores the therapeutic nature of play, suggesting that it can rejuvenate our mental well-being at any age. Through insights from neuroscience, developmental psychology, and personal anecdotes, Dr. Brown demonstrates play's critical role in intellectual growth, social interaction, and overall happiness. He also cautions against a society devoid of play and passionately advocates for its continuous presence in our lives.

Marcel underscores the necessity of setting aside time exclusively for play with all of his athletes. He opines that both coaches and athletes should allocate periods solely for spontaneous play.

This doesn't imply sidelining structured drills and practices. Instead, it's about weaving in sessions where athletes can revel in their sport, devoid of any pressures.

Ironically, early specialization can inhibit versatility. Athletes exposed only to specific drills for their main sport miss out on the broader athletic development that comes from diverse play. This may result in a limited skill set that can be a hindrance at higher competitive levels. As discussed in previous chapters, predicting the trajectory of sports evolution in the ensuing decade is challenging. Consequently, shaping athletes who can effortlessly adapt to shifting dynamics becomes crucial.

Marcel lists five pivotal elements he believes are markedly bolstered—ensuring sustained success for athletes—when play and joy are accentuated during their formative years.

Enhancing Motivation

Athletes who derive genuine joy from their pursuits are fueled by intrinsic motivation: the innate desire to engage in an activity purely for the love of it. Such motivation often leads to enduring commitment in sports. Rather than placing their focus solely on external validations, like trophies and rankings, athletes set personal, smaller goals. These might include mastering a new technique, setting a personal best, or simply enjoying a match with friends. These personal milestones fortify an athlete's connection to the sport, ensuring prolonged involvement.

Such personal connections ensure sustained participation. Moreover, teams that share enjoyable experiences often foster better communication, understanding, and trust. In team sports, group training sessions that prioritize enjoyment can lead to stronger bonds among members. Off-the-field camaraderie often translates into superior on-the-field performance. The heightened motivation from these positive experiences ensures that young athletes remain engaged, fostering a competitive environment for all involved, even if their immediate motivation isn't to win.

In general, athletes who genuinely relish their sport and derive happiness from it are more intrinsically motivated, which in turn correlates with persistence, dedication, and long-term commitment—factors pivotal for success.

Reducing Risk Factors of Stress/Burnout and Avoiding Injuries

One of Marcel's signature sayings is, "I'd take a bad training session over a good injury any day." This wisdom, which he first acquired from Leif Olav Alnes, the current coach of Karsten Warholm, underscores the significance of preventing injuries. But it also emphasizes the importance of making training enjoyable and diverse. Incorporating fun activities can break the monotony of rigorous training, serving as a protective measure against both burnout and dropout, especially in young athletes. Marcel's multifaceted background, which includes training with the national sprinting team, participating in exercises with the national bobsleigh team, and playing soccer and handball in the second league, has endowed him with a depth of experiences like hardly anyone else. This positions him uniquely, equipping him to tailor training regimens for a wide range of athletes.

Marcel is a vocal advocate against early specialization, citing athlete burnout as a severe repercussion. Pushing children too rigorously toward a single focus can lead to both physical and mental exhaustion, causing them to lose their passion or even abandon the sport altogether. Athletes who delight in their sport are less prone to such burnout and typically enjoy longer careers. While occasional off days are natural, a consistent pattern can signal an impending injury or burnout. It's essential to recognize that preventing injuries is pivotal for early athletic development.

Introducing elements of joy and fun into training can rejuvenate athletes, infusing their sessions with renewed vigor and enthusiasm.

While injuries are an inevitable part of sports, incorporating fun activities can serve as active recovery. These activities help athletes relax and rejuvenate after demanding training or competitions. A positive mindset is also vital for swift recovery from setbacks and failures. Athletes with this outlook tend to see challenges as learning experiences rather than threats, bolstering their resilience. One crucial aspect is adopting a playful approach to focus on strengthening weaknesses, which will benefit the athletes in the long run. Moreover, positive emotions and overall happiness confer health benefits, such as a fortified immune system and expedited recovery times. As a result, a contented athlete might face fewer health issues and rebound more promptly from injuries.

Coping with Pressure: Building Mental Resilience

Enjoyment during training often transforms into confidence in competition. Athletes who relish their practice sessions tend to have more faith in their abilities. Given the immense pressures, particularly at elite levels, it's essential to prioritize athletes' mental well-being. Regular check-ins, dedicated mental training, and ensuring they have pursuits beyond their sport can help strike a balance between intense training and relaxation. Positive emotions can sharpen athletes' focus, enabling them to effectively filter out distractions, concentrate on the task, and make optimal in-the-moment decisions. Furthermore, fun can serve as a shield against the stress and tension inherent in high-stakes competition. Athletes in a positive frame of mind are better equipped to manage stress, mitigating the detrimental effects of stress hormones on their performance. Marcel recognizes that not all sports benefit from the same approach. He emphasizes that in disciplines requiring short power bursts, like powerlifting, technique and rhythm are also crucial; however, the mental resilience in these sports often involves mobilizing a different kind of energy, which can be more beneficial for executing the lift.

"Pirre Nyskjerrigheten": Sparking Curiosity, Creativity, and Skill Development

In an environment where play and enjoyment are prioritized, mistakes aren't just tolerated; they're embraced. To some extent, these errors can even be the most enjoyable part of the process, and athletes might actively seek them out. In such a setting, everyone is learning and enhancing their abilities. This kind of environment is optimal for skill acquisition. When training emphasizes exploration and enjoyment, athletes are encouraged to try out new techniques without the fear of failure. As sports techniques and even rules continue to evolve, it's crucial for young athletes to have a diverse set of tools acquired from various activities. This foundation will enable them to adapt, learn, and explore new techniques throughout their careers.

Overall Well-being and Holistic Development

Joyful experiences in sports allow athletes to develop not just as players, but as individuals. They cultivate values such as teamwork, leadership, and discipline, which benefit them in and out of the sports arena.

Marcel's list reads not just as a blueprint for success, but also captures the very essence of the success model. Norway seems to grasp this intuitively. From athletes' earliest days, enjoying nature over their structured sports training, the element of fun has always been a constant. This aligns with the growth mindset: the belief that abilities and intelligence can be cultivated through dedication, hard work, and a persistent sense of playfulness. It's not surprising that they not only achieve excellence but, perhaps more importantly, savor the journey toward it.

The road to mastery is filled with challenges, including long hours of intense practice, moments of self-doubt, and the relentless pressure to improve. Yet, when this journey is infused with fun, challenges transform into intriguing puzzles, setbacks become valuable learning experiences, and the entire endeavor takes on the nature of a game.

The Norwegians have a distinct appreciation for "joy in sports." This concept, deeply embedded in their sports culture, stands in contrast to the more absolutist and command-driven models found in other nations. Their unique blend of "play" and "friluftsliv" encourages curiosity without limitations. Norway's approach strongly correlates happiness with achievement. While it's important not to generalize, there's no denying that this mindset has birthed remarkable talent within the country. When this spirit of free exploration is dynamically balanced with structured, rule-bound competition, the result is a valuable ingredient of the Viking Code.

The Viking Code places importance on recognizing Norway as a nation that emphasizes collective values and unity. Moreover, it understands that organized sports aren't solely about individual excellence. They serve as a platform to forge community bonds, enhance social skills, and instill values like discipline, resilience, and mutual respect. When young Norwegians glide down snowy slopes or compete in team sports, they are not merely playing; they are preparing for life.

Within this life-long journey, the element of fun stands as a cornerstone of learning. The games we engage in, and the joy derived from them, don't just mold our skills. They shape our attitudes toward challenges, growth, and how we view life's journey. This ethos isn't only evident in elite athletes like Warholm, Haaland, and Hovland. Across Norway, on every training pitch, you'll find parents, coaches, and role models infusing fun into training, fostering skill acquisition, and cultivating a growth mindset.

A significant part of this ethos is rooted in a distinctive Norwegian cultural trait. Something that we truly can refer to as "*typisk Norsk*"—typical Norwegian—and this is our final ingredient of cracking the Viking Code: the "dugnad."

But before we discuss the "dugnad," we'll meet Martin Ødegaard.

Martin Ødegaard—One More Pass

In a tucked-away corner of port city Drammen, on a field—referred to as "Løkka" by Norwegians—a boy of merely 14 plays soccer as the chill winds of October sweep across. The Norwegian soccer season is nearing its climax, and most of the nation remains oblivious to the diamond in the rough that is Martin Ødegaard. But unbeknownst to them, the murmurs had begun, reaching as far as the German powerhouse soccer club, Bayern Munich.

When confronted by the media about the rising whispers of interest from the European elites, Ødegaard responds with the kind of measured calm not often seen in kids his age. "They won the champions league so right now they are the best club in the world. They play good [soccer] with many good players," he comments. His boyish appearance belied the depth of his aspirations, which were cast toward those very Champions League nights.

Locally, many had an inkling about Ødegaard's flair on the pitch, but few anticipated a meteoric rise to the top of Norwegian soccer. Yet, as whispers transformed into deafening chatter about this exceptional talent, Ødegaard soon found himself stepping onto the top-division stage. In only the third game of the subsequent season, at 15 years and 117 days, he took to the pitch against Aalesund, cementing his record as the youngest ever in the

Tippeligaen. Amid the seasoned professionals, young Ødegaard, wearing the Number 67, made the intricate art of soccer look as breezy as a child's game. "Walking onto that pitch, I couldn't wipe the smile off my face. It was an opportunity, and it felt exhilarating," he remarked post-game.

Amid the pulsating rhythms of the game, as young Martin danced past a handful of the most experienced players in the league, the world caught a fleeting glimpse of the promise that lay ahead. By the time he had masterfully crafted an assist and delivered some of his awe-moment passes, spectators, both in the stadium and in living rooms across Norway, sat a little straighter, feeling the unmistakable ripple of something transformative. After that display, his coach, Ronny Deila, tried to encapsulate this budding genius: "He has an understanding of the game that has unique and extreme technical skills, but the most important part is he has great value on a solid foundation. He is a grounded boy that simply just loves to play." After that display Ødegaard was soon at the top of the wish list of almost all European clubs.

But Ødegaard was just getting started. Soon, he'd made history again as the youngest ever goal-scorer in Norway's top-flight soccer. Yet, amid the swirling storm of growing fame, Ødegaard was out marching in the nation's May 17th parade alongside his schoolmates. The media, now entirely enamored by this wunderkind, followed his every step. In an almost cinematic moment, a young friend, innocence shining in his eyes, ventured closer to the mic, declaring, "Mark my words; he's destined to be the world's greatest [soccer player]."

On a cold December day in 2014, as snowflakes might have lazily wafted down on parts of Europe, Martin Ødegaard celebrated a milestone. His 16th birthday wasn't just a personal rite of passage; it marked a pivotal shift in his soccer journey. Now he was legally eligible to enter the grand theater of European soccer.

Martin's footsteps had visited training grounds of some of Europe's soccer cathedrals: the fierce energy of Liverpool FC, the ambitious dynamism of Borussia Dortmund, the rich history of VfB Stuttgart, the artistry of Barcelona, the methodical precision of Ajax Amsterdam, and, not to be forgotten, the storied might of Bayern Munich. Each club visit was not just a testament to Ødegaard's skill set, but also a clear indication of the unfolding tug-of-war for this Norwegian sensation.

In the middle of speculation and anticipation, Karl-Heinz Rummenigge, the soccer titan steering Bayern Munich, didn't just add to the rumors; he amplified them. Facing the press with his characteristic directness, he announced, "We're pulling out all the stops to secure Martin. And in this chase, I believe Bayern stands more than a fighting chance." The stage was set, and the world watched, waiting to see where this young maestro would sign.

Fast-forward a decade, Martin Ødegaard's name shines along-side, Erling Braut Haaland, on the nominee list for the coveted Ballon d'Or. Out of 30 of the world's best soccer players, Ødegaard secures an illustrious spot. Still only 24, with the weight of the captain's armband for both his club (Arsenal, where he's led them to top of the league) and his national team, it's evident that Ødegaard's journey from "Løkka" in Drammen to the global stage was no fleeting moment of brilliance; it was the heralding of a soccer era.

Ødegaard's early part of his journey, however, was not a linear rise to the top; it was a decade of loops, turns, and detours. What set Ødegaard apart wasn't just his talent, but an almost impish, boyish love for soccer. He brought a refreshing maturity on and off the field, paired with an infectious playfulness. He seemed to dance with the ball, inviting everyone to partake in his joy, making seasoned soccer professionals sit up and scribble notes.

Not much past his 16th birthday, he was ensconced in the grandeur of the Santiago Bernabeu stadium, the heartbeat of "Los Blancos." After a whirlwind of speculation, Ødegaard had chosen Real Madrid, the apex predator of European soccer, as his playground. The very idea was the stuff of daydreams for countless young players worldwide. On May 23, 2015, at age 16 years, 5 months, and 6 days, Ødegaard became the youngest player ever to don the white jersey of Real Madrid; he had an entry right out of a silver-screen narrative. In an emblematic changing of the guard, it was the legend Cristiano Ronaldo who, while making his exit, passed on his best wishes to the debutant.

But life at such heights is never easy. Madrid's constellation of stars eclipsed Ødegaard's playful brilliance. The global stage, which should've been his dance floor, felt constricting. Between 2017 and 2020, he was shuttled across European clubs, loaned out to sharpen his skills. At Herenveen and Vitesse, the weight of the "next Messi" tag seemed to pull him down. For any other young talent, these Dutch clubs might have been an excellent platform. But Ødegaard wasn't just another talent; he was a Real Madrid wonderboy.

The tide turned at Real Sociedad. The boyish charmer was back. Regaining his touch, he transformed into one of La Liga's elite midfielders, even challenging his parent club. Sociedad, often a footnote, emerged as a genuine threat to the top echelons, all with Ødegaard at the helm. Then, as 2021 dawned, and still just 22, a new adventure arose: Arsenal awaited the Norwegian maestro.

Six and a half years at Real Madrid, punctuated by a mere 11 appearances, felt like an eternity. Every athlete's journey has chapters, and as the Madrid chapter closed, a new one opened in North London. Arsenal, a club with a storied history and an insatiable hunger for resurgence, saw in Ødegaard the hope for a new leader.

When the Gunners secured Martin's signature in August 2021, they weren't just adding a player to their roster; they were making a statement, a declaration that Arsenal was ready to shape a team around the talents of the wonderboy. The club had been missing a certain creative flair, a spark. And in Ødegaard, they found the ember that could ignite a firestorm. His impeccable vision, precise passing (a staggering 91% accuracy during his initial Premier League outings), and ability to maintain possession were nothing short of mesmerizing.

Yet, it's essential to look beyond just numbers. In Ødegaard, Arsenal saw a leader for a new generation. Alongside the dynamism of Bukayo Saka, the verve of Gabriel Martinelli, and the raw talent of Emile Smith-Rowe, Ødegaard was not just a player; he was the nucleus. Their collective might even give giants like Manchester City a run for their money in the race for the coveted Premier League title.

Their manager, Mikel Arteta, himself a master of the game in his playing days, recognized the nuances of Ødegaard's play. Arteta became both a mentor and guide, helping him navigate the rigorous waters of the Premier League. This synergy between a budding superstar and a manager with keen technical insight felt serendipitous. Although they fell short of Premier League glory in their first season, there was an air of anticipation. Ødegaard, with Arsenal embroidered on his heart and his squad by his side, was just getting started. Their appetite has been whetted, and the world awaited their encore.

In the quiet moments between games, in the hallowed halls of press rooms, the world often glimpses an athlete's essence. When Martin Ødegaard sat with the *Telegraph*, we saw not just a soccer player, but a young man wrestling with duality. "Everyone has this perception of me being really nice and calm all the time," he said, but as he spoke, layers unfurled. "But I am a different person on the pitch. I get angry; I get frustrated. I have this fire inside of me. I have this passion and this drive to do my best, to win. I want to do everything perfectly. I want to be the best, all the time."

Yet, in another introspective moment, this time with Alex Aljoe, a more nuanced image of Ødegaard emerged. Talking about the revered red and white, the weight of leadership, and Arteta's idiosyncratic management style, we saw the resilient spirit that defines Martin Ødegaard. "There were challenging times," he admitted, adding with an unwavering conviction, "but I never stopped believing in myself, I always kept going."

After a standout season, the humility in his voice was palpable as he acknowledged his evolution, but quickly added, "I can always improve." And as he continued, reflecting on the daily grind, the practices, and the continual strive for that next perfect pass, he circled back to an ethos—an ethos that encapsulates the Viking Code. With a hint of that familiar smile, Ødegaard concluded, "I come in everyday with a smile on my face."

6

"Dugnad": Everyone Participates

ALTHOUGH MY PARENTS are in their 70s, they still step out for an occasional evening "dugnad." Their commitment to the tradition of "dugnad" remains unwavering. Think of a "dugnad" as a form of volunteer work, known in many global cultures, but without the feeling of work—it's not laborious. It's reminiscent of the German concept of "Ehrenamtlichkeit" yet stripped of the "Ehre"—which translates to "honor"—and without the formality implied by the "amt," indicating an official role or duty.

While "volunteer work" may sound strenuous and often feels like something we're obligated to do without pay, a "dugnad" is a heartwarming Norwegian tradition that goes beyond simple community service. It's a dance of solidarity, a testament to the power of collective effort, turning neighbors into extended family members. It is the essence of local sports clubs and community events. For centuries, Norwegians have come together for these voluntary endeavors, be it rejuvenating a communal garden, painting a school fence, or constructing a playground.

The term "dugnad" has its roots in Old Norse. It can be dissected into "dug," meaning "help" or "good deed," and the suffix "nad," denoting a period of doing something. Thus, "dugnad" translates to "a time for helping" or "a time for good deeds." It's derived from the Old Norse word "dygð," signifying proficiency or capability. In Old Norwegian, "dugnaðr" referred to an additional effort to complete a task. The term goes beyond the mere definition of "volunteer work"; it embodies the spirit of unity, the joy of shared endeavor, and the collective pride of achievement.

The heritage of "dugnad" is twofold: it's embedded in both the linguistic origins and the longstanding social practices of Norwegians. Historically, due to Norway's rugged landscapes and severe weather, communities had to band together for survival. Whether prepping for the harsh winter or undertaking communal projects like home construction, neighbors pooled resources and efforts. Such collective volunteer endeavors were crucial for both efficiency and fortifying communal bonds. Today, the tradition persists in forms like neighborhood clean-ups, school event volunteering, or fundraising activities.

Beyond its practical role, "dugnad" epitomizes a mindset of collective responsibility, community, and altruism—values deeply cherished in Norwegian culture. The "dugnadsånd" ("dugnad" spirit) emphasizes community support. This spirit manifests not just in work, but also in shared laughter, tales, cups of hot cocoa or coffee, and the tradition of "dugnad buns" or pastries. This setting allows the younger generation to learn from their elders, strengthening bonds and nurturing community essence.

In modern Norway, "dugnads" are omnipresent—often organized by sports clubs or schools. Activities can vary from organizing a festival to painting a clubhouse. While many might envision exclusive clubhouses and luxury cars parked prominently at membership clubs, signifying funds available for ongoing maintenance and service, the Golf Club in Røros is distinct, much like many others in Norway. Its lifeblood is the "dugnad."

As I check in with my parents on the weekend, I find my dad deep into preparing the annual financial statement for the upcoming projects of the local Lions Club. "What are you up to?" I asked. "Litj Dugnads-arbe for Lions," ("Some dugnad work for Lions") my dad replies.

The "dugnad" effort is founded on the principles of voluntarism, with everyone contributing according to their ability. This practice captures the essence of the Norwegian belief that when hands come together and hearts align, extraordinary things occur. It transcends mere obligation; it's a vibrant celebration of unity, a ritual preserving the rich Norwegian spirit of community. "Dugnads" foster a profound sense of solidarity and belonging, demonstrating that collective efforts often yield greater results than individual ones. At its core, the Norwegian "dugnad" spirit is deeply rooted in a strong sense of community and shared purpose.

In an era that leans heavily toward individualism, "dugnad" stands as a testament to the timeless power of community. Central to the Viking Code, it serves as an educational foundation emphasizing "togetherness." At its core lies the concept of "medmenneske." While this Norwegian term can be loosely translated as "fellow human being" in English, its depth is far more profound. It encapsulates the recognition of others as sharing our human journey, underscoring mutual experiences, empathy, and solidarity. This is not just about being grounded; it's about belonging. You are one of us.

A Declaration of Interdependence

"I am because you are." While the American dream emphasizes independence and individual ambition, the Norwegian model seems rooted in an unspoken commitment to interdependence: If you thrive, I thrive alongside you and perhaps even rise further.

As I pen these words on a Sunday, Erling Haaland has netted another goal for Manchester City, solidifying the soccer team's top position in the Premier League, with him as the leading scorer. Later that night, 22-year-old Jakob Ingebrigtsen faces off against elite African athletes from Kenya and Ethiopia in the 5,000-meter dash World Championship final. Battling discomfort, he outpaces his competitors, including Moroccan-born Mohamed "Mo" Katir El Haouzi, in the final moments to clinch the title. On the same day, Viktor Hovland claims victory in the FedEx annual tournament, crowning him the world's top golfer in 2023.

Any given Sunday.

Or in the case of the Norwegian athletes, by now, just another Sunday.

Marcel is preparing Casper for the first match of the US Open. I text Marcel a brief message, wishing them luck. He promptly replies with a Portuguese "we are ready" and that we will have a chat later in the week: "nós estamos prontas 💪." I suggest we meet on Tuesday after the match, assuming he wins: "😉 👍." As I await further reflections from Marcel, I turn to a book I've marked up with sticky notes, curious to contrast the unity of the Viking Code with the American Dream's individualism.

In *The Upswing: How America Came Together a Century Ago and How We Can Do It Again*, renowned American political scientist Robert Putnam, best known for *Bowling Alone*, provides an in-depth exploration of societal shifts. He chronicles America's transition from a period of intense polarization and stark inequality in the late nineteenth century to a more communal and equal society in the twentieth century, before witnessing a decline during the turbulent 1960s.

Using a mix of statistical data and engaging narratives, Putnam traces the societal journey from an "I" to a "we" orientation and its subsequent reversion. Drawing from historical reform movements that redirected America's trajectory, he suggests ways in which today's society can reignite its communal spirit.

In exploring the potential framework of a "Viking Code," an intriguing pattern emerges. Beyond individual successes in varied disciplines lies the power of the collective. Perhaps even more deeply, there's a universal appeal for unity as a foundation for nurturing individual talent and unveiling latent potential.

Norwegian life isn't solely about advancing individual prowess; it prioritizes fostering robust, supportive communities. The "dugnad" principle exemplifies collaborative effort, illustrating how one can excel as an individual while simultaneously contributing to and thriving within the community. Pairing scientific insight with Norway's communal ethos suggests that perhaps our focus should shift to a "Declaration of Interdependence." This would emphasize a shared set of foundational values, forging a resilient core. It's compelling to think that with this refocused approach, we're entering a transformative path.

As we began the second part, diving into the journey of self-trust and the belief in surpassing any previous benchmarks to unlock hidden talents, we end the first part with what serves as both a reminder and inspiration, echoing the core values of the Norwegian ethos: Even if you excel, you are still "one of us."

Throughout these chapters, it's evident that many factors contribute to outstanding performance: hard work, dedication, and even external factors like lifestyle and maybe even weather have played roles in shaping these world-class athletes. Are we observing a fleeting phenomenon of a younger generation of elite athletes, emerging resiliently like coltsfoot through the pavement? Or are we witnessing a blueprint for cultivating high-performance cultures and revealing latent talent?

Our exploration of "dugnad" represents the final piece in deciphering the Viking Code. I want to conclude my discussions with Marcel and focus on how the "dugnad" spirit intertwines with high performance and the essence of the Viking Code.

While Marcel has worked with individuals to meticulously navigate the intricacies of high performance, emphasizing the perfection of daily habits, he still views "dugnad" as a core principle when fostering a united group. Working collectively toward a shared goal often achieves outcomes greater than the sum of individual efforts. This principle is not only foundational in team sports, where success hinges on a united effort, but it also underscores how community spirit and togetherness play crucial roles in the journeys of individual athletes.

The principles of collective effort and unity have shaped a model where individuals are encouraged to contribute, becoming integral parts of the local ecosystem, thereby enabling others to flourish. Marcel firmly believes that individual success is closely intertwined with collective effort. When one person excels, it often ignites the motivation in others, elevating the overall performance of the group and paving the way for more individuals to succeed. This camaraderie and team spirit, which is nurtured through participating in "dugnad," is deeply embedded in the DNA of Norwegian high-performing athletes.

Marcel also ties the concept of "dugnadsånd"—the spirit of "dugnad"—back to our earlier discussions on shared responsibility. In a "dugnad," every participant owns their part of the task. This deep sense of commitment is mirrored in high-performance settings, where the dedication of each individual culminates in a collective triumph

Interestingly, Marcel draws a parallel to the historical significance of "dugnad," which was crucial for communities to endure the long, severe Norwegian winters or to reconstruct after disasters. This fostered a deep-rooted sense of resilience and grit. Marcel believes that this resilience is not only a hallmark of high performance across various domains but also a key component of the inner fortitude seen in modern Vikings. Such intrinsic motivation—fueled more by a genuine passion and love for their sport than by external rewards—often results in heightened levels of performance and dedication.

Across various cultures, there are concepts that celebrate communal voluntary work: "toloka" or "tłoka" in countries like Russia, Ukraine, Belarus, and Poland; "talkoot" in Finland and the Baltics; "harambee" in Eastern Africa; and "gotong-royong" in Indonesia. In South America, numerous terms encapsulate the spirit of community and voluntary effort for the collective good. However, having grown up in Norway—and not merely out of patriotism—Marcel and I firmly believe that the "dugnad," an enduring element of Norwegian culture, is a crucial ingredient that plays a role in our sports successes. In 2004, "dugnad" was even recognized as the "national word of the year" and celebrated in a television program aiming to pinpoint what is "typically Norwegian." Fast-forward 20 years, and the children born around the turn of the millennium are now dominating in numerous sports disciplines, far surpassing our established excellence in winter sports.

The significance of "dugnad" goes beyond the immediate task. It serves to strengthen community ties, instill trust, and foster a sense of belonging. This was poignantly demonstrated during the collective fight against the coronavirus. While there was also criticism of politicians and the dissemination of information in Norway, the nation adopted a distinct communication strategy. Following the outbreak's announcement on March 12, 2020, Norway rallied behind a "nasjonal koronadugnad"—a national "dugnad" against corona. This united front positioned Norway favorably in many global evaluations of pandemic responses, as the country embraced a cohesive approach. In essence, the prevailing sentiment was "I am because you are"—by banding together, we all thrive.

Similarly, in high-performance settings, a sole focus on results can be counterproductive. Adopting a holistic approach that encompasses team bonding, mental well-being, and personal growth often leads to better outcomes.

While "dugnad" isn't explicitly a high-performance model, its inherent values and principles can be seamlessly integrated into high-achievement contexts. This is especially true in environments where teamwork and collective spirit are paramount. However, as we've now learned, it also forms a core foundation in the evolution of individual athletes.

7

The Viking Code: The New Oil

As YOU CAN see from Chapters 1–6, the Viking Code isn't a simple, step-by-step model. Instead, it represents a holistic development stemming from both deliberate efforts—a nation deeply dedicated to sports and high-performance culture—and factors that might have serendipitously contributed to its success. Understanding these elements is vital for those hoping to emulate this achievement.

For years, I've observed the steady rise of Norwegian athletes— these modern Vikings who've conquered some of the world's most challenging sports arenas. In a nation of merely 5.5 million inhabitants, the extraordinary success and sheer number of top-tier athletes indicate there's more at play. Beyond their remarkable achievements against intense global competition, I've been particularly struck by their grounded demeanor, widespread popularity, and the respect they command from teammates, competitors, and the media alike.

A standout aspect of early development in the spirit of the Viking Code reveals a profound truth embedded in Norwegian culture: it is considered irresponsible for parents not to foster the physical development of their children. Essentially, it's a call to action: Get up. Get out. Move. It's about "doing," the act of engagement. However, upon analyzing the traits of these athletes, several common characteristics emerge, summarized in this chapter, that reflect the essence of the Viking Code and lay the groundwork for the development of a new culture of high performance.

Work Ethic and Unconditional Will to Progress

While victories are celebrated, these modern-day Vikings are never content. Their hunger isn't for fame or fortune, but for progress. Their training ethos mirrors their competitive spirit, with meticulous attention to detail, acknowledging the importance of recovery, and utilizing the latest in sports technology. Their mantra is simple: pursue excellence with an undying passion for sport. A predominant trait is their unwavering focus on continuous improvement. As they begin to specialize—after acquiring a diverse skill set and a broad "toolbox"—their coaches, mentors, and often their fathers emphasize that success hinges on persistent positive development.

Handling Expectations, Pressure, and Nervousness

Ambitious athletes must navigate the external pressures and expectations. Striking the balance between triumph and defeat often depends on their mental fortitude. These athletes exude self-confidence without arrogance. Many view nervousness as a catalyst, channeling their anxieties productively. Interviews often reveal how they harness fear, refining their routines to ensure they relish every competition.

Love for the Game and Playfulness

While parental support is a recurring theme, there's a consistent message: don't take yourself too seriously. Emblematic of this sentiment is a quote I came across from runner Karsten Warholm:

"We don't cure cancer; we're here to have fun. Sport isn't important, but we choose to make it important."

Positivity

An unwavering belief in the power of positivity resonates among them. To garner broader interest in sports, negativity is a deterrent. Their attitude mirrors a principle: rather than lamenting what they lack, they lead with optimism and action, embodying what seems to be a shared Norse motto: Show up and act.

Respect

They deeply value their achievements without complacency, consistently lauding their competitors and recognizing that everyone who reaches the global stage is exceptional and deserving of accolades.

For Norwegians, it's crucial to remain true to the principles that have shaped their success rather than seeking proven methods elsewhere. The current generation of standout athletes has been inspired by pioneers across various disciplines who pushed boundaries and expanded Norway's cultural horizons. While these athletes will undoubtedly inspire future generations, it's uncertain whether this level of success can be sustained indefinitely.

Building a high-performance culture is complex, and this complexity only increases when there's a limited pool of individuals to draw from. Infusing this culture with core values introduces a myriad of internal, external, and ethical factors. However, when properly understood and adapted, the Viking Code has the potential not just to remain a sustainable model for Norwegian success but also to inspire other nations worldwide to develop their interpretations of these norms.

However, *The Viking Code* book goes beyond the triumphs of Norwegian athletes and the prowess of young "modern Vikings." After extensive conversations with one of the leading coaches and drawing from my own experience in professional sports, I've come to view the Viking Code as an untapped reservoir, akin to newly discovered oil from a seemingly inexhaustible source. It can serve as a catalyst for progress and prosperity, not only reviving the spirit of hard work and high performance in various aspects of human life but also imparting a deeper meaning. Perhaps it even holds the key to fostering collective endeavors aimed at addressing the most pressing challenges of our time.

In my quest to unravel the underlying narrative of Norway's success, I've reflected on its broader implications: Could the corporate world, the education sector, and politics glean insights from this Norwegian blend of peak performance and fundamental values? Can the Viking Code offer a roadmap for tackling pressing global challenges, whether it be climate change, technological advancements, geopolitical conflicts, poverty, or societal divisions?

It is now time to bid farewell to Marcel, move away from the gold-crowned triumphs, the sweat, and the tears of professional sports, and to address how the Viking Code might resonate with leaders in politics and business.

Could the philosophy of the Viking Code even be a blueprint for a fairer, more ecological, and prosperous society?

PART

II

The Viking Code as a Practical Philosophy

ON NOVEMBER 22, 2022, I had the honor of being invited to speak before a group of top executives and politicians at the Royal Norwegian Embassy in Paris—*La Norvège en France*. The event was hosted by Ambassador Niels Engelschiøn and Svein Tore Holsether, the president and CEO of Yara, a global leader in fertilizer production.

To some, Yara is a behemoth of the climate crisis. Yet, the company is spearheading a new mission: the pursuit of climate-friendly fertilizers and emission-free energy solutions. It's a narrative that challenges preconceptions—that economy and ecology aren't contradictions but an essential, inextricable symbiosis.

Yara's mission, ambitious and laden with challenges, echoes the themes of the Viking Code. It is about pushing boundaries, yes, but doing so with a deep-seated respect for the collective well-being. In its endeavor, Yara isn't just looking to revolutionize its industry; it is redefining the relationship between profit and planet.

The conversations that day were not typical corporate fare. They were infused with a sense of purpose, a commitment to a cause greater than the bottom line. As Holsether spoke, his words manifested the ethos associated with Norway—a blend of ambition and responsibility, of striving for excellence while being acutely aware of one's footprint on the world.

The gathering was further graced by the presence of a hedge fund manager, an art collector, and a particular individual who gained notable recognition in 2019. This individual, Nikolai Tangen, was celebrated by the *Sunday Times* as one of the United Kingdom's most generous millionaire philanthropists. In May of that same year, Nikolai, along with his wife Katja, pledged their commitment to the "Giving Pledge"—a philanthropic campaign initiated by billionaires Bill Gates and Warren Buffet, designed to encourage the wealthy to donate half of their fortunes for the betterment of others.

Nicolai Tangen, with his distinctive Norwegian-English accent and always on the go with his backpack, epitomizes the image of the modern Viking: always moving, constantly active and bustling. His birthplace, Kristiansand, is quaint and hardly hints at how he was able to conquer such an extraordinary position. As the head of Norges Bank Investment Management, he oversees the Norwegian State Fund—the world's largest sovereign wealth fund. This fund, created in 1990, is the cornerstone of the Norwegian economy, born from the bubbling surpluses of the country's oil sector. Its aim is to invest the current revenues from Norwegian oil and gas production for the long term, preserving them for future generations' post-oil era. To this end, the fund invests globally in a wide range of assets, including stocks, bonds, and real estate. Under Tangen's dynamism, this fund flourishes: with assets of an impressive 1.34 trillion euros, this amounts to about US$250,000 per Norwegian citizen. In other words, being born in Norway doesn't mean starting with a deficit, but with a quarter of a million from day one. Of course, this is symbolic, and it's not money one can personally spend, but it speaks volumes about the collective distribution of resources. "Oljefondet"—the Oil Fund—belongs to the citizens of the country.

Traditionally, the CEO of the State Fund operated behind the scenes, but Tangen shines in the public eye. His podcast, available on platforms like YouTube and Spotify, has stirred attention. Tangen is somewhat of a modern influencer. He educates on corporate affairs and entrepreneurship, enlightens on climate and sustainability, and provides behind-the-scenes insights as he converses with leading figures in business and media. Approachable, down-to-earth, yet purpose-driven, he advocates for a new ethos of performance by sharing his perspective on hard work and his values with the public. He reaches out to young people, the general public, investors, and entrepreneurs alike. Sometimes, he's seen in sports attire reminiscent of soccer star Erling Haaland; other times, he's discussing tech giants like OpenAI founder Sam Altman, or exchanging ideas with luminaries like Bill Gates and Elon Musk. Viewers get the impression: Tangen is one of us, yet a leader who stands out, carrying an entire community with him, in line with the principle of "dugnad."

Tangen challenges the Law of Jante. He consistently upholds the belief that success is achieved through hard work and dedication. He keeps an eye on the bigger picture but remains grounded in his short-term micro-ambitions, appreciating the process and the small moments that lead to the realization of these ambitions. Meeting him is like a brief plunge into a whirlpool of ambition and inspiration.

Through his actions and words, Tangen embodies a defiance of the traditional norms, yet he does so by weaving his individual success story into the larger narrative of collective progress. He is a testament to the potential within the Viking Code—a symbol of how individual drive and community spirit can coalesce into a powerful force for change. His story is not just one of financial acumen but a broader narrative about leadership, influence, and the transformative power of reimagining success. In Tangen's world, success is not just measured in balance sheets and stock valuations but in the impact one can make on society and the environment.

As I reflected on Tangen's approach, it became increasingly clear that the principles of the Viking Code have relevance far beyond the boundaries of Norway. They offer a blueprint for a world seeking to balance ambition with responsibility, profit with purpose. In a landscape often dominated by short-term gains and narrow perspectives, Tangen's vision presents a refreshing contrast—a reminder that true success lies in the strive toward harmony of individual achievement and collective well-being.

And yet, it's not just through listening to his podcasts that another side of Tangen becomes apparent. One can sense a human warmth, a grounded connection to his fellow beings, and a profound understanding of the weight of responsibility he carries.

Tangen manages to strengthen his personal brand while consistently emphasizing the values of the collective. And this brand wields power. Companies in which Tangen invests through the Norwegian State Fund are acutely aware that any misstep—whether in terms of climate or ethical values—could lead to a loss of reputation in today's media landscape. This is not only because Tangen openly addresses these shortcomings but also because he doesn't hesitate to withdraw funding, significantly impacting the stock value.

His approach is a blend of traditional Norse wisdom and contemporary global awareness. Tangen understands that true leadership extends beyond financial success; it's about shaping a better world, where economic prosperity coexists with ecological responsibility and ethical integrity. He stands as a beacon, not only leading his companies toward profitability but also steering them toward contributing positively to the planet and society.

The Viking Code also finds its expression in diplomacy and politics, exemplified by Jens Stoltenberg. His tenure as NATO secretary-general since 2014 isn't merely a series of dates and decisions. It's a series of challenges woven from global tensions, the incorporation of new members into NATO, the recurring question of relevance echoed in Trump and Macron's remarks about NATO being "brain dead," and, of course, the critical issue of Ukraine post-conflict. Stoltenberg's time at NATO is defined not just by these events but by his relentless pursuit of unity amid crises and uncertainty.

Stoltenberg possesses a keen sense of cultural respect and tact. In his public statements, he consciously chooses to say "Türkiye"—as the Turks themselves pronounce it—instead of "Turkey." This might seem a minor detail to some, but in the world of diplomacy, where every word is meticulously chosen, it sends a powerful message. This subtle yet significant choice is more than linguistic accuracy; it's a sign of respect, intuition, and the art of communication—qualities that Stoltenberg has consistently demonstrated as an embodiment of the Norwegian value system deeply ingrained in its diplomacy. Through numerous meetings, his approach to communication helped alleviate tensions surrounding the induction of new NATO states, Sweden and Finland. Turkey and Hungary, which complicated processes with their vetoes over several sessions, were eventually persuaded.

The essence of the modern Viking—or the Viking Code—is reflected in every facet of society, from high-stakes diplomacy to playful learning apps. In the second part of this book, we will explore whether the values embedded in the Viking Code can provide us with the tools to tackle some of the most pressing challenges of our times. I firmly believe that this Norwegian philosophy could offer a roadmap for progress in business, politics, education, and society at large—a blueprint for our shared future and thus for the continuation of organized human life.

Practical Implications of Ancient Philosophy

In the intricate web of today's economic and political systems, shaped by structures of power and knowledge, we often yearn for clarity and simplicity. The Viking Code is not a cure-all, nor does it claim absolute truth, but it offers a clear direction for an enlightening philosophy. I am aware that Norway—like any culture or entity—is not without its flaws. Even as you read these lines, developments may unfold that reshape the perception of Norway and the Viking Code. Perhaps a new scandal has emerged, or the fundamentals of the Viking Code are being tested by unforeseen challenges.

However, this book aims to crystallize the positive aspects and chart a course for ongoing refinement and positive progress. As a Norwegian, I hope my compatriots continue to reap the benefits of the Viking Code. But my vision extends beyond that. As a citizen of the world, a European, and an integral part of Germany, my interest transcends the boundaries of my homeland. I find myself pondering how the insights of the modern Viking Code can lead us all toward a better and united future.

The journey of understanding and applying the Viking Code is not static; it is dynamic and ever-evolving. It is about harnessing the principles that have shaped Norway's path and adapting them to the global stage. This philosophy is not about imposing a singular worldview but about finding common ground in our diverse experiences and aspirations.

The Viking Code is neither a secret training method nor a miracle diet. It's also not a collection of ancient runes etched on a weathered stone. Rather, it's a timeless philosophy for life, a kind of compass providing direction amid the overwhelming complexity of our modern world. It draws inspiration from the minds of continental philosophers whose thoughts have shaped not just continental Europe and my work over the years, but the entire world. From Socrates, Kant, and Nietzsche to Theodor W. Adorno and Hannah Arendt—their insights equip us to view the Viking Code in a global light, as the triumphs of the modern Vikings resonate with the ancient philosophical wisdom.

A modern interpretation of ancient wisdom, blended with the Viking Code, offers a unique perspective and can help us become thinkers of *our* time. It suggests that success and fulfillment are not just about reaching specific goals or milestones but about the journey toward a more balanced and enriching life. The Viking Code, therefore, is not just about navigating the challenges of the present but about building a legacy for the future—a legacy that combines the best of our past with the possibilities of our future.

Therefore, we want to find out if the Viking code, derived from the observation of sporting success, possesses a "magic" that we can transfer to other areas and from which we can learn beyond sport.

And so we come to the core of this book: Do we find inspirations also in education, politics, and economy, which are also results of a cultural ethos? Can we take something from sports for our everyday life on a global scale and work together on a positive future for our humanity?

8

The Viking Code in Society: One World Education

IN ANCIENT GREECE, two institutions embodied the vision of a united world: Zeus's Olympia, symbolizing the Olympic spirit, and Plato's School of Athens—the Academy. Both envisioned a coming together, whether to play, compete, learn, or understand. While the Olympic spirit endures, the essence of education seems to have faded.

On September 28, 2022, I spoke at TechPoint, a leading technology conference in Kristiansand, Norway. It was one of those flawless autumn days, a harbinger of winter, inviting one to savor the moment.

Here, where everything felt different from the usual, I met someone backstage who was also different: fellow Norwegian Johan Brand. He's a fascinating blend of a modern lumberjack and a Nordic sailor, inspired by the marine exploration pioneer Jacques Cousteau, reincarnated in a contemporary hipster style. Dressed in a cream-colored blazer paired with the historic and symbolic orange cap, reminiscent of Cousteau, he exudes confidence, intelligence, and creativity. When Brand enters a room, you feel it. Clear and poised, he radiates the energy of the Viking Code. Beyond his seafaring appearance, Brand also harbors a genuine passion for the ocean. He talks about the Blue Economy, and one of his two sailboats is even named *EntrepreneurShip*, underscoring his belief in teams coming together onboard to discuss the next big project. Alongside Swedish management professor Robin Teigland and entrepreneur Anita Krohn Traaseth, we engaged in a panel discussion after my speech about technology, sustainability, climate, and leadership.

This gathering at TechPoint was a modern-day "School of Athens," where knowledge, ideas, and visions for the future converged. It was a testament to the Viking Code's relevance in today's world—a world increasingly interconnected by technology and global challenges. The spirit of the conference was not just about technological innovation but also about rethinking how we educate, lead, and sustain our world.

Johan's approach exemplifies the Viking Code in action. His blend of entrepreneurship, environmental stewardship, and team collaboration mirrors the values of the Viking Code—the pursuit of excellence, the importance of community, and the responsibility toward the environment. His leadership style, combining adventure with purpose, echoes the essence of the Viking Code in a modern context.

The discussion, moderated by media creator Per Valebrokk, was particularly captivated by Brand's journey. Just a few weeks earlier, I had stumbled upon his work in the field of education— particularly in EduTech, as it's called today—without realizing that we would soon meet on stage in Kristiansand. Brand is the cofounder of Kahoot!, a learning platform that has revolutionized education.

"We want to make learning awesome," Johan often remarks.

His boundless enthusiasm has propelled Kahoot! from a university project in Norway to a global phenomenon. Johan and his cofounders envisioned creating a global classroom. Over the years, classrooms around the world have demonstrated the importance of creative and experience-based learning that fosters a deep understanding of challenges, as students celebrate "epic victories" after solving complex problems on the platform.

Kahoot! focuses on collaborative learning and incremental progress. While much of its content is created by students, the platform is grounded in state-of-the-art technology. It's a space where pop culture meets education, exemplified by remixes like rapper Snoop Dogg's interpretation of the Kahoot! melody.

Today, Kahoot! is present in 200 countries and regions; in 2022 alone, the platform and the Kahoot! app reached eight million teachers. Half of all US teachers, 97% of Fortune 500 companies, and top universities worldwide use Kahoot!, which is an incredible success. Since its inception, the platform has registered more than 9 billion plays, and more than 200 million Kahoots have been hosted.

This success story is a testament to the Viking Code's principles of collaborative achievement and continuous learning. Kahoot! not only exemplifies technological innovation but also a commitment to educational advancement—a core aspect of the Viking Code. It's about creating environments where learning is not just an individual pursuit but a collective experience, where technology serves not just as a tool for information but as a catalyst for engagement and understanding.

As Johan spoke about Kahoot!'s journey and its impact, it became clear that the Viking Code can indeed manifest in various forms—in this case, through an educational platform that transcends traditional boundaries and encourages a more inclusive and dynamic approach to learning.

The story of Kahoot! is more than just a business success; it's a narrative about how a vision, rooted in the values of the Viking Code, can lead to profound societal impact. It highlights how the principles of collaboration, innovation, and shared knowledge can reshape the educational landscape, making learning a more engaging, inclusive, and effective experience for learners worldwide.

A technology start-up, born in Norway, bolstered by a $200 million investment from Asian giant Softbank, and licensed in Hollywood with Disney-themed apps, now finding its place at the heart of global education? Who could have predicted such a trajectory?

What's the secret behind this modern Viking success story?

What does it really mean to "make learning awesome"?

Kahoot!'s ethos has always centered on the playful element, reminiscent of the Viking Code: it needs to be fun. "We use play as our first language," one of the company slogans goes. At Kahoot!, the focus is on the collective experience. The learning platform is designed to create "campfire moments"—instances where the focus shifts from what you learn to how you learn. The platform and its ethos aim to engage "the learner in all of us," mobilizing heart, hand, and mind.

In education, encouraging learning, or positive reinforcement, is crucial. This principle, which is also central to the Viking code, is what Johan Brand sees as a key factor for the success of Kahoot! Just as athletes perform at their best amid cheering fans, students thrive when nurtured by supportive mentors—formerly simply known as teachers—and celebrated by their peers. The ethos? When one succeeds, we all triumph. By recognizing individual successes and promoting collective progress, an environment is created where students are stimulated to discover, learn, and assert themselves. Kahoot! has essentially introduced the applause of joy into the classroom.

Johan Brand possesses the innate ability to quickly grasp the essence of problems. In line with the Viking code, he once invited his biggest competitor onto his sailboat. Today, they are not just allies, but also friends, united by a common endeavor: to address and solve a global problem. Their collaboration reflects the spirit of "dugnad."

Now, Brand has embarked on a new venture to realize the construction of a research and education institution at the bottom of the Oslo Fjord. Imagine an upside-down terrarium where people learn about the sea. His goal is to lead "det grønne skiftet"—the green shift, the transition to more sustainable and environmentally friendly practices—and to promote "den blå økonomien" or the "blue economy." He wants Norway to take a leading role in the sustainable use of marine resources, to create economic growth, improved living conditions, and jobs, while preserving marine ecosystems.

But his dedication to education remains unbroken.

Through his company "we.are.human," founded in 2010, he delves into the intricacies of human development. His investment strategy? He bets on ROL, return on learning, a refreshing contrast to the traditional ROI (return on investment). Johan, the modern Viking, is a living testament to the durability of the principles of the Viking code.

From the Knowledge Society to the Society of Understanding

We have transitioned from the industrial revolution to an era characterized by hyper-productivity and maximum efficiency. Our educational models have been designed to produce experts who accelerate optimization and keep pace with societal development. Now, the focus is shifting to the nuances of human traits and the subtleties of organized human life, diverging from what technology cannot yet achieve. We are moving from a rigid and absolute knowledge society to a society of understanding.

But what are the implications of this shift for education?

In an era shaped by AI, we are returning (or being forced back) to the fundamental principles of education. In a world where infinite knowledge is freely accessible, we no longer need answers—technology provides them—but rather profound and better questions. The rise of AI forces us to rethink education itself and the path to it. True enlightenment does not begin with absolute answers, but with the quest for truth. The knowledgeable differ from the wise, the truth proclaimers from the truth seekers.

Is there any sense in grading tasks when students can effortlessly and flawlessly complete them at home using AI tools? Should the strategy of educational institutions be to fight against AI and invest in tools that can differentiate between human-generated and machine-generated content? What is fundamentally the purpose of school? Should children still learn handwriting in an age of digital communication? Is its purpose to prepare students for the unpredictable journey of life? Are students adequately prepared for an ever-evolving economic landscape? Many questions now need to be answered.

Futurist Sinead Bovell presents a simple perspective shift in rethinking our educational paradigms. Faced with the challenge that students use AI for homework at home, she suggested a changed perspective: "Perhaps what used to happen at home should now take place in the classroom." If we assume AI creates "perfect" tasks everywhere, the focus should shift from mere knowledge reproduction to fostering deeper understanding. Instead of simply creating the task at home, students should critically analyze, refine, and even question AI-generated content during their school time without AI tools. This shift underscores a fundamental return to the essence of education. It's not about producing experts with rote-learned knowledge, but nurturing learners who understand the art of learning itself.

The renaissance of reason and understanding harks back to the lively discussions in the ancient Agora and suggests that a new and global educational model is needed today. The foundation of the Agora was the promotion of analytical thinkers, united by a common ethos. In our interdependent global community, a model for such a "global classroom" seems necessary. In line with the principles of the Viking Code, it emphasizes enhancing human potential and producing powerful individuals who prioritize values and collective well-being—as well as shared successes. Although this vision may seem idealistic, its harmony with the Viking Code suggests its great potential. Just as joy and progress are paramount for athletes, so is learning in education. It's not about (absolute) knowledge, but about the perception and joy of insight.

When we think about what I refer to as "weltbildung" (One World Education), we must even take the paradox of bridging human evolution and artificial (general) intelligence into account. What are the actual implications of merging mensch with machine? What may sound like science fiction is in fact a unification of mythos and enlightenment. Or in the sense of Socrates, everything conceivable is achievable.

How should we understand this?

We are in the process of creating omniscience through the rapid progress of exponential technologies. At the same time, we are confronted with seeking "the new" and continuing our journey of creation. Over the next 10 years, as the technological tsunami grows stronger, we will have to ask ourselves: "If we are given the powers to create everything imaginable, what future would we build?" In other words: "Which future is worth striving for?"

It would be interesting to explore to what extent a "perfect AI" will enlighten humans through absolute knowledge so that we could free ourselves from dogmas and all "connected" people would have the same starting situation.

However, to avoid slipping further into technological utopias or dystopias, we return to a point that makes clearer the challenges we face today: It's no longer enough to simply claim that humans can now focus on "the essentials" thanks to technology. We must now clarify what the essentials actually are.

The knowledge society model fits seamlessly into today's optimization narrative. While we have optimized our world, it seems to have been at the expense of our planet and social cohesion. The rapid spread of information reflects the hurried and immediate gratification culture we have cultivated in recent decades. Regrettably, many governments seem to lack the courage to face this new reality.

Although scientific discussions about these changes continue, many have been surprised by the speed of change. Yet the most transformative wave of technological advances is still to come. We are at a turning point in human history, where we are both forced to determine our path and have the means to do so. Fundamentally, humanity has never been so ready to shape a future worth living. And that is exactly what we expect from our educational models today. We are ready now. We have the foundations and the technology. Education must now "future." It must explore the world and have the will to truth as its foundation.

The Illusion of the Knowledge Society

The dream of a universal classroom is alluring. However, in many state education systems, the focus is merely on "digitizing" schools by incorporating new technologies into outdated learning paradigms. Imagine a classroom: students, full of enthusiasm, each equipped with the latest AI-driven device. Their growing self-confidence convinces them that they are receiving a first-class education. Yet, when they step into the real world, they discover a gap between theory and practice, between aspiration and reality. Not in their knowledge, but in their understanding.

Up until today, education systems have been like conveyor belts producing standardized minds. But why? Why do we insist on teaching every child in the same way and at the same pace? As a father, I often wonder: Why this curriculum? Why this method? Education should be more than just memorizing facts.

With the vision of a global classroom comes the model of a different school. A school not structured like the factories of the industrial revolution, but as an open space reflecting the breadth and diversity of the world. No more barracks or prisons, but open fields of discovery. In this school, students are not just numbers; they are curious explorers.

American philosopher Richard Rorty believed in an educational approach rather than an epistemological one. He saw education as a bridge between cultures, epochs, and disciplines. It's about connecting dots, recognizing patterns, and embracing diversity. As Rorty aptly stated, the goal of education is "to lead us out of our old selves and help us become different beings."

In Rorty's vision, great educators are not just systematic, but primarily transformative thinkers. They question norms, break barriers, and inspire wonder. They see the world in all its complexity and embrace its contradictions.

With the digital tidal wave hitting our education system, we need nothing less than a paradigm shift in education that values the beauty of not knowing as much as the pursuit of knowledge. Like another American philosopher and science historian, Thomas Kuhn, who described the paradigm shift in sciences, we are now at the threshold of transformative change in education. Kuhn posited that a new paradigm emerges when the prevailing paradigm exhibits too many anomalies and can no longer provide satisfactory explanations. The current education system, heavily reliant on deductive learning, faces numerous challenges in meeting the diverse needs of learners in a rapidly changing world.

The "old model" of deductive learning, where a teacher summarizes the contents of a book and then the student dives into the chapters to see the details for themselves, has already been replaced by an inductive model. The existing school system was built around a structured path, guided by a predefined narrative or theory and seeking evidence to match it. In a deductive learning environment, general principles or theories are introduced first, followed by specific examples to support or explain them.

This was the classic "top-down" approach, where the teacher as an expert imparted knowledge and students passively absorbed it. The inductive model, however, works from the bottom up—changing modern pedagogical approaches as a new way of learning. Here, learners start with specific observations or experiences and then draw general conclusions from them. This method is more exploratory and practice-oriented, often connected with real applications, problem improvements, and discovery-based tasks. It is the thrill of discovery, the educational journey, connecting dots from different sources, which forms a larger picture. Students themselves delve into a source, approach texts and concepts, and build their own competence. The teacher acts as a guide but also helps clarify misunderstandings and consolidate knowledge. The concept of competence moves away from competence as something static. Instead, it expands and deepens by encountering concepts anew, but in different contexts. Outside of school, learning is often already inductive. The anomalies of the old model have now been exposed, and the call for a holistic educational paradigm grows louder—a paradigm that integrates various learning styles, including inductive, experiential, and collaborative approaches, and ensures that students are not just recipients of knowledge but also creators of knowledge, active participants in their own educational journey.

The new educational model—One World Education—is based on exploration and curiosity, while the old seeks clarity and validation. The magic happens when both models are intertwined, when technological advancement merges with human potential.

In contrast to a truly educational society, our current knowledge society stands. The rise of this society has not necessarily promoted deeper learning but simply shaped the era of optimization. The increasing importance of science has unintentionally diminished the value of a holistic education. Metrics like citability, popularity, and financial success overshadow the genuine pursuit of truth, creating a confusing paradox that clouds our perspective: the pursuit of the usability of our findings leads away from the pursuit of knowledge.

Over the last half-century, we have unintentionally created a dangerous information ecosystem. Amid this dense thicket of data and information, technology attempts to create a realm anchored in pre-validated, factual knowledge, where humans only have to react and function. This change is one of the greatest in human history, and it will revolutionarily influence our understanding of what it means to be human in the coming decades, with the rapid advent of artificial intelligence and the unlimited access to (free) knowledge. In the coming decade, the marginal costs of intelligence and thus of knowledge will tend toward zero, thanks to a technology-driven ubiquity. The sheer speed and intensity of this change became palpable for many with the emergence of AI platforms like ChatGPT. Who among us can imagine GPT 7, 9, or Version 11 or artificial general intelligence within the next 3 to 4 years?

Turning Away from Fragmented Knowledge

How did we even arrive at this absolutist knowledge society? A widespread misconception is that elevating (scientific) knowledge inherently enhances the value of education. However, our fixation on facts, theories, and established norms has led us astray. We are trapped in a relentless information society, sustained by the ambivalence of technology and our unwavering belief in absolute knowledge.

In today's world, education is hailed as a symbol of prestige. Calls for strengthening education are everywhere, yet the deep essence of the term seems to have evaporated. We live in a society inundated with knowledge, but one must ask: Is it truly enlightening?

"We wish to serve history only to the extent that it serves life: for it is possible to value the study of history in such a way that life becomes stunted and degenerate," wrote Nietzsche. He warned of the dangers of over-emphasizing history to the detriment of life. His words echo today, as we face a flood of data but thirst for true insight.

The digital age heralds a new enlightenment. With AI and its tools like ChatGPT, the knowledge of the world is just a few keystrokes away. Yet, even though data are more accessible than ever, a society of understanding remains a vague goal on the distant horizon. Our modern educational institutions, once recognized as centers of wisdom, resemble a mirage that has drifted far from its fundamental ethos. Today, we venerate static knowledge and neglect the dynamic nature of true learning. Contemporary universities may be technologically advanced and pillars of the knowledge age, but they have strayed from the true core of genuine education.

Once lauded as bastions of critical thinking, our educational institutions now resemble assembly lines producing graduates who are competent in their fields but often ill-equipped to navigate the subtleties of the world. These "fragmented specialists idiots," as I would call them, shine in their specific areas but remain isolated from broader societal contexts.

Historically, the term "idiotes" in the polis referred to individuals who kept away from public-political engagements. Today's specialized experts, ensconced in their knowledge silos, exhibit a similar distance. They find comfort in their niche expertise and hesitate to venture into the broader public sphere, fearing the world's vast complexities. This narrow knowledge offers an appearance of stability but also restricts them. When they venture out, they often react defensively, trapped in their own certainties.

Such an approach not only limits their perspective but also impedes true understanding and, most importantly, progress. This excessive dependence on standardized knowledge has led to a society that, despite possessing knowledge, often lacks enlightenment.

Immanuel Kant's definition of enlightenment is particularly apt here:

> Enlightenment is man's emergence from his self-imposed immaturity. Immaturity is the inability to use one's understanding without guidance from another. This immaturity is self-imposed when its cause lies not in lack of understanding, but in lack of resolution and courage to use it without guidance from another. Sapere Aude! Have the courage to use your own understanding! is thus the motto of enlightenment.

The democratization of knowledge is undoubtedly a positive change enriching our global community. Yet while access to information has never been easier, true understanding seems more elusive than ever. This newfound abundance of knowledge can be a double-edged sword. We often treat our acquired knowledge as the ultimate truth and become prisoners of our beliefs and unrecognized assumptions. Standardized through our academic endeavors, we view the world through a single lens, solidifying our perspectives. We risk a kind of uniformity that turns every discourse into a closed event.

This narrow focus blinds us to the countless ways to approach the world and makes us complacent in our beliefs. We risk losing sight of alternative viewpoints, which hampers a dynamic understanding of our surroundings. This intellectual tunnel vision not only limits our worldview but also endangers our intellectual autonomy. We become bound to our acquired knowledge, allowing it to dictate our perceptions and actions.

Kant's words warn of the dangers of an excessive dependence on fragmented knowledge. Today's "expert idiots" often lead their followers into a labyrinth of their own certainties, confusing narrow perspectives with universal truths. The "filter bubble" is not just a digital phenomenon; it manifests in our entire educational approach, and it is no coincidence that it is precisely this category that is rapidly replaced by AI. Where we have a lot of information and are precise, AI starts. Data processing and storage capacity are now the strengths of the new knowers. The human expertise is on the brink of a fall.

In these times, Kant's call for enlightenment resonates deeply, urging us to use our minds courageously. While our society is inundated with information, we must beware of echo chambers that distort reality. Knowledge, as valuable as it is, must be balanced with dynamic understanding. If knowledge becomes a mere commodity used more for economic leverage than for genuine human growth, we risk losing sight of the true essence of education.

Education should be more than just a means to employment or a status symbol. It should ignite curiosity, foster creativity, and impart a deep understanding of our multifaceted world. And it is here that the Viking Code enters as a guide to an educational philosophy. In our pursuit of a continually evolving understanding of our dynamic world, the micro-ambitions of education are key to testing and overcoming perceived boundaries, to give direction to the dynamics of the world that should advance our team—humanity. Only education that focuses on understanding rather than mere knowledge transfer allows us to play the infinite game—to "future."

The knowledge society, emerging from a technology-driven era, has often pushed individuals into predefined paths. This model, prioritizing economic growth, directs individuals onto a regulated educational path that culminates in a conformist life. Such an approach stands in stark contrast to the ideals of enlightenment, but also to those of the Viking Code.

At its core, education should benefit the individual and foster harmonious societal interactions. To improve our societal structures—and capitalism in a broader sense—we must begin with a paradigm shift in education. It is a "dugnad" that promotes the collective and brings forth confident and self-aware learners through the educational philosophy itself. People who understand growing with others and also commit to the collective—humanely.

The Virtue of Not Knowing and the Art of Being Wrong

Imagine a world where the brightest minds come together, not to flaunt their knowledge, but to celebrate the beauty of the art of being wrong. In this world, it's not about reciting facts but about the journey of learning itself.

Today, we are stuck in a paradox. We live in a knowledge society, yet hesitate to admit our mistakes. It's a race for affirmation, for the ego, to be right. But what if true education lies in embracing our ignorance? The philosopher Hans Blumenberg once noted that appreciating science does not mean devaluing education. Science opens a window to the world, but it's only a piece of the puzzle. Specialized knowledge, as valuable as it is, can sometimes blind us to the bigger picture. It's like having a map but no compass; you know where you are but lose sight of the direction.

At the heart of the Viking Code and modern Viking athletes is an insatiable quest to uncover ignorance. It's not about fostering a culture of failures, but about creating a high-performance culture where the goal is to explore more to achieve progress. And it's in this view, where not knowing becomes an art form, that the power of progress lies. The art of being wrong shapes the core of progress in the Viking Code.

Ultimately, education is not about what is thought or said, but about thinking itself. How we think about the world. That is education. The task today—it seems to me—is to engage with a knowledge society where no one wants to admit errors. A defense of one's facts and the manifestation of one's opinion—the absolutization of "knowledge"—we experience from the breakfast table with our family to the worldwide web. It's about fame, roles, voices, and ego. We have optimized and maximized the "art of being right" with the consequence of absolute division and leading meta-debates (debates about the debate), which we postulate as freedom of opinion. Far from the truth-seeking nature, we are today postulators of half-knowledge. We are trapped in our own certainties.

In this fast-paced world, we often forget the beauty of pausing, of introspection. But challenging times have a way of holding a mirror up to us. They remind us that true growth comes from a mix of expertise and humility. It's about recognizing one's own limits and transcending them. Learning the word, whether in written form or spoken, must be understood as thinking. It's the spirit of what I call the "professional amateur."

Zen Buddhism introduces us to the concept of "shoshin," the beginner's mind. It refers to an attitude of openness, eagerness, and lack of preconceptions when learning, even at an advanced level, as a beginner would. It is the mindset of the early starter who becomes the uncatchable, as exemplified by Norwegian athletes. It is the art of seeing the world with open eyes, free from preconceptions. It is the wisdom of Socrates with his, "I know that I know nothing." In a society obsessed with expertise, there is a deep power in embracing our inner beginner.

Hannah Arendt spoke of "natality," the idea that each birth brings a new beginning. We come into this world unformed—with an empty storage— ready to be shaped by experiences. The broader these experiences, the later the specialization, the deeper the pursuit of knowledge, because the desire, the joy in it grows. It's a dance between the world and us, where we are constantly shaping and being shaped. This dynamic balance is the heart of education and the essence of the lost art of education that strives for progress and better explorations: the art of being wrong.

In a knowledge society, where one's knowledge is equated with education and set as absolute, "uneducation" is the only way to education. If we equate knowledge with education, we must activate the uneducated in us. Why should we do this? The mindset and values of the uneducated distinguish the educated in today's knowledge society. The need to grow, the critical approach to what exists, and the curiosity and openness to the other are the attributes that distinguish an educated person. But these attributes have lost their significance in the knowledge society, where one's knowledge is set as absolute.

The fetishization of knowledge, as Theodor W. Adorno, one of the main representatives of critical theory, characterizes the so-called half-educated person. The half-educated have acquired the same knowledge as educated people, but the half-educated do not understand how to grasp phenomena in their vitality. Instead, they approach phenomena mechanically. The half-educated are rigid in their thinking and knowledge. They do not understand how to fit knowledge into larger meaningful contexts. Instead, it is about half-digested knowledge for its own sake. Education thus becomes an attitude, a mere sign of social belonging in our society of self-optimization. The mere fetishistic collection of highlights of intellectual knowledge replaces penetrating understanding from concrete, factually motivated interest in the world. Such education is rigid, without dynamics and liveliness.

For Adorno, education signifies a tension or dialectic between spirit and adaptation—between the intellectual independence from social or natural constraints and the mutual involvement of people in shaping their living conditions. We need knowledge, but we also need not knowing, openness in every respect— intellectual openness. This dialectical tension is now strongly dominated by the side of adaptation. There is a fundamental imbalance.

Education is consequently characterized by a dynamic balance. This allows us to become and to facilitate the process of change. Education is thus a constant becoming. For this, rigidity and dynamics are required. We need rigid knowledge as well as critical handling of knowledge and openness to the new, the other, the independent. The latter characterizes the uneducated. We must strive to educate ourselves. But at the same time, we must not lose the attitude that comes with "uneducation." Only the attitude of uneducation ultimately leads to education. Uneducation and education thus stand in a dialectical relationship to each other.

Education is an open process. It is permeated with worldliness. Through the world, we become. In dealing with the world, development takes place. We educate ourselves, but we never reach an end. We will never fully understand the world or ourselves. But this should not stop us from striving for it.

The widespread trend of awarding numerous bachelor's and master's degrees brings to light a fundamental contradiction. How can one "complete" something that is inherently infinite? This conundrum arises from a misinterpretation of the nature of education. Both Humboldt and Arendt saw education as a continuous journey, not a destination. To use Hans Blumenberg's eloquent formulation: "Education is not a depot; it is a horizon." Education is the infinite horizon that cannot be "reached" like a fixed point after a set travel time and passing certain milestones. This horizon is as wide and boundless as the world itself.

Perhaps our task and responsibility are not to provide a framework for training creativity, but to not untrain the innate ability that comes with "natality." With this, we find ourselves at the core of the Viking Code.

From this perspective, education is, on the one hand, mastering the game, and on the other, cultivating the playing, which we have come to know as an integral part of the Viking Code. It becomes clear that the concept of an educational degree, which now shapes the understanding of education with the inflationary bachelor's and master's degrees, is a contradiction in itself. This is only possible in a world where we have not understood what education really means.

Education must not be understood as something finite. It must therefore be understood as something infinite.

The guiding concepts are emancipation and autonomy. In particular, the educational concept of the Enlightenment was, as a "motor of emancipation," a prerequisite for the "emergence of man from his self-imposed immaturity." To illustrate the essence of true education, the American linguist Noam Chomsky draws on the response of a long-time MIT colleague who was asked by first-year students what they had to cover in their first semester: "It's not important what you cover, but what you discover." This simple statement is an invitation to explore, to question, to delve into the unknown.

One World Education: Global Education

When Johan Brand and his colleagues set out to build the "World Classroom," it was a way to unite the world and ignite the torch of a new education system. Such a change is not a "quick fix," but a generational transformation.

I refer to this as creating "better problems" and "positive progress." When I say "better problems," I mean freeing ourselves from old certainties and self-evident truths that are absolute and have a final solution. It's understanding the complex dance of life, realizing that not all problems are the same. "Better problems" are not just bigger challenges; they are markers of growth, the kind you encounter when you've ascended. In a world where "growth" was associated with the economy and numbers from an external perspective, the inner growth and growth of humans have not been equally explored.

"Better problems" signify that you've overcome yesterday's hurdles; essentially, the presence of better problems is a testament to your progress.

"Positive progress" is not just about moving forward; it's about becoming better. "Positive progress" is measured not only in milestones but in the quality of the life journey. It's a type of progress that enriches, building on both quantity and quality. It's progress that considers not just the individual, but also the community, the environment, the bigger picture. In a world obsessed with speed, "positive progress" is a reminder that direction is as important as distance.

The essence of education is learning how to learn. It's about awakening and fostering curiosity, as Marcel repeatedly addresses in the first part of this book. It's the desire to understand the world and our place in it.

At the heart of learning, there's also a social aspect that expresses great satisfaction in doing something with others and being seen by others. It's about the playful aspect of competitiveness, where one feels present and alive. Ultimately, education should bridge the gap between people and provide an explanation for the empty spaces. It's about empowering people to think, reflect, and grow.

What's next?

I firmly believe that we need not just a global classroom but a global perspective, which I call One World Education, or "Weltbildung." It's not just about institutions; it's about a mindset, a philosophy of life, in which we develop the Olympic spirit of Zeus for a global renaissance of enlightenment, placing learning at the center of life, and taking the collective ethos of the Viking Code as a guiding principle, where the individual can grow through the collective.

This infinite amplification of "positive progress" can be our desirable future. An educational model that, at its core, is the same for 6-year-olds and 60-year-old board members of a global company. It's a model that is rooted in ancient philosophy, which today becomes a practice of thought—a practical philosophy—where we all become thinkers of our time.

Only by freeing ourselves from the limits of the familiar can we truly understand the world and our place in it and develop an educational philosophy whose horizon is the world with all its contradictions, simultaneities, and the unknown as the basis of our educational institutions. It's a model based on analytical thinking, enjoying complexities while simultaneously finding beauty in simplicity and perfection, that pursues the forward-looking micro-ambitions that allow our daily conscious experience; a model where we continually strive to be unattainable, in the tradition of "dugnad" pooling our strengths for a common goal; a model that emphasizes the playful lifestyle of Johan Brand and the team at Kahoot! and the essence of the Viking Code.

The path where one evolves from a "truth preacher" to a "truth seeker" is set by modern technological society. For me, the role of education is to make us individuals who can find their own way in society. For children currently in educational institutions, learning social skills and self-confidence is the foundation for going out into the world and acting.

The Viking Code, combined with a new global educational initiative, similar to the vision of a digital global classroom—a One World Education model—is the path to an educational philosophy and a society of understanding that, using technological possibilities, leads us into a world of progress.

9

Change Factor: The Viking Code Meets Politics

SONDRE RASCH COULD be described as an "ultranerd." By the age of 12, through delivering newspaper and doing housework for others, he had earned enough money to buy his first used computer for 300 euros. Inspired by his gaming community, he recognized the need to set up servers for others and developed his first business idea—right from his childhood bedroom. Today, however, Rasch no longer lives in the mountains along the rainy coast of Norway but runs his companies from San Francisco. Independent of the global wave of home-office work that arose during the COVID-19 era, Rasch moved to Palo Alto with a visionary idea. In January 2016, he became part of the renowned incubator network of Y Combinator. Just 8 months later, he managed to win Sam Altman as an investor. His company changed its name from Konsus to Superside and began offering creative services through a global network, providing cost-effective and rapid top-notch services from all time zones. Their vision: to integrate the top 1% of creatives worldwide and offer their services through this global network. Rasch and his team focused on "remote work"—working from anywhere—and were rewarded for it.

Today, globally networked work is indispensable. Safety Wing, one of Sondre Rasch's newer companies, emerged as an evolutionary development of his worldview and represents an unusual business idea: a health insurance specifically created by and for digital nomads. Traditionally, a company has a location. The conditions at the location determine the framework for service production, not only in terms of infrastructure but also in terms of labor law, tax law, and social legislation. When a company detaches itself from the physical location, it also detaches itself from those reference points that made local or regional politics relevant. Rasch has recognized a development that applies not only to a globalized economy but also to personal and national identity and, consequently, membership in a political framework. He has realized that the range of services, including care and security measures, could also shift into global competition. A young, active, and high-performing part of society might increasingly turn away from state offerings to develop and use new, globally attractive options, a development that could put severe pressure on the state's product and service catalog. The providers of services are looking for alternatives, while those who predominantly draw services may be left behind—in an increasingly pressured "father" or "paternity" state. The *Digital Nomads Report* by MBO Partners (2023) reports that already 17.3 million people in the United States identify as digital nomads—people who are part of local events but work as global citizens everywhere and are globally networked. The study also shows that 72 million Americans think about becoming digital nomads in the next 3 years. And these are just the US numbers. However, this trend is not limited to the hipsters of Silicon Valley and similar hotspots.

Similar developments are also seen in Europe and other parts of the world. Safety Wing offers these constantly traveling digital nomads, who often have no firm ties to their home country anymore, a straightforward and globally valid insurance solution. Rasch describes this idea as a response to a personal problem: on his travels, he found no company willing to insure him globally without a fixed address.

Sondre Rasch ventures a—in your eyes, perhaps steep—thesis: "With high probability, this decade will produce a network on the Internet that can factually be considered the first country—a network state—with state functionalities. And that's what our company is now preparing for."

If this is true, how will the power dynamics of our world change? Currently, political movements and politically legitimized bodies are empowered through more or less representative elections (at least in Western democracies) to shape the conditions for human coexistence through laws. The Internet and worldwide networking are eroding this power because they offer those who are intellectually or financially capable the opportunity to escape the politically set framework. This is the factual termination of a social contract.

To what extent is that still democracy?

Heading to New Shores: The Upcoming Digital Democracy

Democracy, in its origins, is a form of government that derives its legitimacy from allowing all members of society to participate in the political decision-making process. If we consider democracy as a living entity currently undergoing an identity crisis, how can it evolve without compromising its core—without exposing its vulnerability?

Can traditional parties steer this evolution?

If we take a look at the world democracy ranking, Norway often sits at the top as a crown jewel. Is this "perfect democracy" and the flourishing of Norway merely the result of an oil-fueled economy? Or was there already a democratic ideal in the country's institutions, just waiting for an opportunity to manifest itself?

Democracy is normally viewed as a static system—a homeostasis. German sociologist/philosopher Niklas Luhmann, Chilean biologist/philosopher Francisco Varela, and Chilean biologist/philosopher Humberto R. Maturana argue to replace the concept of homeostasis with homeodynamics. In the case of social systems, stasis is rigid and static; it is stagnation and thus simultaneously the death of a (self-regulating) system. Homeodynamics, on the other hand, is infinite and dynamic, adaptive, and characterized by its recurring emergence and adaptation. More than 20 years ago, French philosopher Jacques Derrida described how democracy should be understood in times of globalization, technology, and hospitality. He spoke of the "democracy to come"—la démocratie à venir—a democracy that is constantly becoming. Is Norway's secret understanding democracy as a dynamic and adaptive system that finds its way in time?

The "democracy to come" does not refer to a specific or future political order. Rather, it is an ethical ideal or a constant task, something fluid. It is a democracy that is never fully realized but always exists as a goal to be strived for. Derrida's philosophy will shape the future. It is oriented toward creation and coincides with the philosophy of the Viking Code. It is not subject to homeostasis but rather to homeodynamics.

For Derrida, democracy shows itself in the following:

- **Imperfection:** Democracy is always imperfect and unfinished. This means it must constantly be questioned, revised, and redesigned.
- **Openness:** The "democracy to come" must be open to the unexpected, the other, and the new. This contrasts with fixed or final political systems that do not allow for change.
- **Critique and self-critique:** Constant criticism and reconsideration of an existing democratic system is encouraged to expose its flaws and limitations.

■ **Indeterminacy:** Like many of Derrida's concepts, the "democracy to come" is deliberately vague and undefined. It is more an orientation than a fixed goal.

Derrida argues that true democracy is always in motion and constantly changing. It exists in a permanent tension between the current state and what could be possible. Referring to democracy, we come to a significant insight: while a bureaucratic, inflexible state apparatus and a rigid union, rooted in their self-satisfaction, lacking openness to the new, and showing a lack of willingness for self-criticism, desperately search for leaders with clear identity, vision, and creative energy, digital nomads and innovators dance and celebrate their own visionary future arts.

What is possible?

Can we technologically transform the fundamental concepts of democracy?

Can we simply move away, or is there a possibility to influence the functions and services of our elected representatives?

The core of my thoughts is the question of what kind of society we, the citizens of a country, want to shape. What can we agree on? At this point, we return to the essential substance of shaping—to power. It's about a forward-looking vision for an interdependent world. We have the options for progress open to us, positive, unlimited progress. Instead of settling for static answers and solutions— "I know, and I am right, that's how it is"—we can now strive for better explanations and better problems.

A simple example illustrates this idea: While Germany struggles with bureaucratic hurdles and digital processes seem far off, Ukraine, even under the pressure of Russian aggression, has developed into a digital hotspot. In collaboration with American technology companies, the RedDot Design award-winning Diia app was created. More than 20 million Ukrainians are already using it to access government services. Mstyslav Banik, head of eServices development in Ukraine's Ministry of Digital Transformation, expands new processes and partnerships almost weekly.

During my visit to Kyiv in autumn 2023, I was impressed by how easily digital documents were integrated into the state portal, Diia, and the variety of services on the Diia web portal and mobile app. Everything is digitally available—driver's licenses, vehicle registration documents, tax returns, and much more.

Weeks later, at a business event, I shared my experiences about the trip. In the evening, I found myself on the couch next to one of Germany's media moguls. We discussed how media creators, business leaders, and politicians must now come together to accelerate change and tackle bureaucracy in Germany. He was enthusiastic about the app I shared with him, and after a few clicks, he turned to me with a characteristic, sympathetic laugh: "Look, Anders, this was even financed by Germany and the EU. . . ." Indeed, the app was realized in compliance with EU technology and design regulations—financially supported from Germany.

Amid the war, Ukraine took on a role as a digital pioneer and other countries, such as Estonia with their eGovernance focus, are adapting the solution, but not an advanced industrial country like Germany.

"I know some authorities and states in Germany that are interested, but others are not," Banik says. He doesn't want to be more specific. "A general problem is that governments don't have competition," he tells German Handelsblatt in an interview and continues, "If a company doesn't want to modernize and offer better service, it goes under. Governments don't have to fear any competitor."

At least that was the case until today.

And that's exactly where the problem lies.

Governments didn't have to fear a competitor because that wasn't envisioned in the traditional understanding of a party democracy. The state, steered by the government, had a monopoly on offers for the citizens. Alternative offers do not come up in a static view of the political will-formation process. Governments "jog"—or in some cases walk—on their track and fail to recognize how on the adjacent tracks, other runners are setting out to overtake the long-standing champion at sprint speed—and do so using the increasing possibilities, both locally and globally. A competition is brewing—we could train for it. This is where the space for peak performances opens up.

We live in an era where we can determine the fate of the human species concerning climate, conflicts, technology, and poverty alleviation, and this also affects how we want to organize ourselves in the future—our "politics."

The key is technological progress coupled with human growth.

We are at a crossroads. Will we turn toward unity and prosperity, or will divisions only intensify as the pages of history continue to be written? It's time to redefine "politics"—organized human life—not as passive administrators, but as proactive shapers of our collective fate. If democracy is understood as "rule by the people," it becomes clear that all members of a community should be seen as a team. Then shaping means integrating high performers as impulsive team players—with the goal of letting everyone play and together achieve better performances. The joy of the game itself—the playing—and a progress-oriented culture—a positive progression—are based on micro-ambitions, to continuously and steadily improve the conditions and framework of the game, to create "better problems" for the people. Thus, democracy in the sense of the Viking Code is positive progress, progress "in the making," which coincides with Derrida's "democracy to come."

Technology and progress no longer thrive exclusively on the fertile ground of freedom. This centuries-old belief faces its biggest challenge. If prosperity can flourish without total freedom, as in the Chinese model of controlled capitalism, what then is the true value of freedom? It's as if we suddenly realize that the rules of the game no longer apply. The chess game of global politics has added a new piece, and we must rethink all our strategies.

But we are blessed with creative power.

Therefore, I firmly believe that despite the seemingly endless crises, we need a mindset of positive guidelines, a creative world-view that allows room for error. We need a vision that stands for values and performance, not against them, and that sets incentives for behavioral change, beyond mere limitation and regulation. In politics, it means optimizing the finite game—the election campaign—and shaping the infinite play—governing. Both depend on each other and form the basis of a functioning democracy. If you don't optimize the game, you don't get to govern. If you only react to the finitude—after the election is before the election—you can't develop creative power for the infinity.

Is it now time to rethink the global order and overcome the boundaries of the old systems?

Modern democracies with their complex "checks and balances" appear to be caught in a paradox. Is the answer, instead of reclaiming the country, to build new states? Today, national bureaucratic corsets can be challenged by global structures that offer alternatives to the offerings of nation-states. Currency and financial systems, educational models, health, and media are everywhere, thanks to modern technology; parallel societies and alternative offers are emerging, against which the state can only fight with regulations. Why? Global structures are technology-based, operate in direct competition, and thus become extremely effective. The global technological offer is aligned with goals shared with traditional democracies: the welfare of participants. So the question would be: If the "race of nation-states" is too slow, are the high performers building their own Champions League? Would then the collective "dugnad" for the existing structures be a solution, or an unconscious shift into the unknown?

The defragmented structures, the lack of competition, and the increasing pressure from citizens wanting to self-organize, along with a need for a "minimum service" in terms of digital offerings that are not available today, are an explosive combination.

"We know how it can work elsewhere today," we can almost read on the lips of the young digital generation. Unlike in history, where rebellion against the state was the answer, the citizens of the country are looking for an alternative way out, a new—and logical—way out in the "both and": both local and global.

The Power of Power

What if I told you that politics is not about power? Surprised? At first glance, it seems contradictory, given our power-driven political landscape. Power in itself is value neutral. It enables design and action. But isn't that exactly what seems to be collateral in current criticism of party politics? Consequently, it appears—at least in perception—not about change, but only about having the levers of power in hand. It's about winning in the finite game instead of playing in the infinite play. A deeper look might be revealing. Is politics leadership, management, or rather a performance art?

Power is undoubtedly present, but is it used for the good of the people? Is it creative power? Our world cries out for innovation and creativity that point the way forward. But when the existing power structure is not open to "the other" or even blocks progress, a dangerous tension arises.

The currency of power was once information—having the crucial knowledge that others did not. Today, it's about the ability to distinguish the essential from the nonessential. All-encompassing knowledge is (at least theoretically) freely accessible to everyone. If politics neglects its creative role, who then fills the gap? The economy?

Here it gets complicated.

A system cannot simply compensate or save another. So, especially in recent times, we see "politics" opening the wallet, crossing fingers, and hoping that its strategy will work.

Until a few months ago, we experienced years that I describe as a "culture of easy money." As a consequence, today we recognize the effects of a change that has not taken this form in history before. If the strategy from the "Father State" fails, what happens then?

Economist Charles W. Calomiris and political scientist Stephen H. Haber make a compelling point in their book *Fragile by Design*. They argue that the dangerous dance between politics and the economy could paralyze both systems.

When we talk about "politics" and "economy" today, we often quickly associate these terms with the construct of nation-states. But this was not always the case. A closer look at our own history and the development of nation-states reveals that they are a relatively young phenomenon in the totality of human history. Many historians view the Peace of Westphalia (1648), which ended the Thirty Years' War in Europe, as a turning point. The principles of territorial sovereignty and noninterference in the internal affairs of other states, established by the Peace of Münster and Osnabrück, are considered the foundation for the modern system of sovereign states.

The seventeenth and eighteenth centuries saw the rise of absolutism through the consolidation of absolute monarchies in Europe, which strengthened centralized control over their territories and laid the groundwork for modern state formation. The French Revolution (1789) was another crucial moment in the development of nation-states. It promoted the ideas of popular sovereignty, nationalism, and citizenship, which significantly contributed to the formation of modern national identities.

The economic changes and the accompanying social restructuring during the Industrial Revolution in the eighteenth and nineteenth centuries created the economic prerequisites for the emergence of modern nation-states. In the nineteenth century, nationalist movements in Europe and America led to the formation of new states and the consolidation of existing states around national identities. Examples include the unification of Italy and Germany, considered significant events in solidifying the concept of the nation-state. The nationalist movements of the nineteenth century were followed by decolonization after World War II.

This wave of decolonization in the twentieth century marked the last peak in the formation of new independent states based on the principle of self-determination and national sovereignty. The emergence of nation-states is closely linked to the development of nationalism as a school of thought, inspiring political and cultural movements aimed at aligning statehood and nation. With their relatively still young beliefs and hierarchies, historically speaking, these structures are beginning to crumble under the pressure of technological upheavals in the twenty-first century.

Imagine a wobbling Jenga tower: each piece you pull out, whether it's a financial mishap, a political controversy, or a technological quake, increases the instability of the tower. This past decade? Many pieces have been removed. Look at educational models, health and financial systems today. These movements are not isolated—they are part of a global trend of lost "leaders," who identify problems but rarely offer comprehensive solutions, let alone understand the profound connections behind the problems. In other words, they do not contribute to improving the problems relevant to the challenges of our time.

Does the ambition in politics to build and maintain power overshadow actual design? If so, there's a risk that citizens in today's technologized world will look for alternatives. Nietzsche mused on the duality of ambition, which can elevate as well as corrupt. His concept of the "will to power" warned of an abyss that uncontrolled ambition could lead to.

In an ideal world, power would be a tool to shape a better future. But its current manifestation, power for the sake of power, appears selfish. A true democracy must strive for a balance between conservation and progress and become an "aspiring democracy." Yet today's political landscape is marked by crises and confrontation. Events such as Brexit, the rise of autocratic leaders, and constitutional crises dominate the news. Currently, we are witnessing the clash of ideologies between East and West. China has grown rapidly in recent years, while the West struggles with the dilemma of freedom versus security.

These considerations show that we face more than just political chaos; a growing gap is emerging between the old powers of the West and the emerging ones in the East. Regions striving to escape poverty challenge the established wealthy, along with their mantra of stable democracies.

In his book *Power: The 48 Laws of Power*, Robert Greene portrays power as a game dominated by manipulation and strategy. Greene's laws, shocking and effective at the time of their publication (1998), now seem more like relics of a bygone era to many young online groups around the world. The narrative appears to have shifted. Today, perhaps more than ever, it's about people before politics. A temporary return of totalitarian leaders characterizes the current media image. But looking deeper, one might ask whether this vision of power—especially among the younger generations—still really resonates today.

The global balance has unmistakably shifted: the East and South are rising, while the West, amid growing nationalist and authoritarian currents, struggles with its own identity. Recall the days of the Cold War. The West's flagship product was its democratic ideology, positioned as an antidote to communism clones like Stalinism and Maoism. The result? The West, led by the United States, with a two-party system, took over a multiparty system, while the East, led by the Soviet Union, committed itself to a one-party state. But despite all the walls and barriers that separated them, the end of the Cold War could not break the long-lasting narrative of "us versus them."

The temporary return of the United States to the global stage under Joe Biden's presidency signals America's attempt to regain its leadership role. However, it was Bernie Sanders—with his now-iconic mittens and folding chair—who stood as a symbol of the stark contrasts in political ideologies. In the United States, Sanders is often labeled as a radical leftist because he advocates for universal healthcare. In Europe, however, such views would firmly place him among the mainstream social democrats. This divergence in perception extends beyond Sanders and highlights the deep divide in political views across continents. It's not about the endless pursuit of progress for people or a truth-seeking performance culture, but simply about power for the sake of power.

While the West grapples with these internal conflicts, emerging Asian countries offer a very different story. It's like discovering an old book that suddenly shines in a new light. With its mix of the Communist Party's monopoly and dynamic economic growth combined with the strengthening of the BRIC (Brazil, Russia, India, and China) alliance, China offers a counternarrative to Western liberalism.

But within this seemingly clear dichotomy lies a multitude of nuances and contradictions. It reminds me of a doctor fixated on a patient's symptoms but overlooking the actual illness. We are in the midst of what some might call a "clusterf*ck," comparable to a complex, Gordian knot. Our current state in global politics? It's a labyrinth where once-trusted maps no longer apply.

While we observe the strain on the institution of the nation-state, decentralized structures and network states seem to be emerging on the horizon.

Why the Revolution Is Absent

The worldwide vibrations of the political stage are today characterized by the swings of populism. Neil Postman, the media critic and cultural pessimist, warned of a different kind of dystopia. He commented,

We kept an eye on 1984. When the year came and George Orwell's prophecy did not come true, thoughtful Americans quietly sang a song of self-praise. The roots of liberal democracy had held. Wherever terror had taken place, we were at least not haunted by Orwellian nightmares. But we had forgotten that there was another vision beside Orwell's dark one—somewhat older, somewhat less well-known, but equally frightening: Aldous Huxley's *Brave New World*. Contrary to popular opinion even among the educated, Huxley and Orwell did not predict the same thing. Orwell warns that we will be overwhelmed by an externally imposed oppression. But in Huxley's vision, there is no need for a Big Brother to deprive people of their autonomy, their maturity, and their history. As he saw it, people will love their oppression, worship the technologies that undo their capacity to think.

In a world dominated by "alternative facts" and the constant flood of social media, perhaps not an obvious revolution is our biggest concern, but the creeping change in how we process information and define truths. The real struggle might lie in the depths of our collective consciousness, and it's time to wake up and fight that battle.

The use of the term "revolution" often implies a nostalgic longing for a bygone era. But in reality, a revolution might be nothing more than a reactivation of old ideas in a new context. Could one think here about dismantling the political tanker into small parts and thus redesigning a kind of "best of" with smaller dynamic units that add up to more than their individual parts?

Did you know that "revolution" originally meant "restoration"?

Even the revolutions of the eighteenth century arose from a desire for restoration. This emphasizes the cyclical nature of societal changes.

Although the French Revolution was a radical break with the existing political and social system, it had many similarities with previous revolutions. Before the French Revolution, other uprisings and reform movements had raised demands for political participation, social equality, and economic transformation. Examples include the various Peasants' Wars in Europe or the English Glorious Revolution of 1688. Their main concerns were the abolition of absolutism and the feudal system and the introduction of democratic and republican ideals. Many of the concepts propagated during the French Revolution were based on the ideas of the Enlightenment, which had gained importance since the seventeenth century. These ideas emphasized reason, individualism, and skepticism toward traditional authorities, leading to a desire for change in the existing orders.

Today, the economy and communication are revolutionizing. They have brought us closer together and enable global collaboration in real time. Interestingly, technology could be both the catalyst for our salvation and our downfall. Just as it connects us, it can also divide us, especially if we allow its rapid development to outpace our ethical and societal norms.

Liberalism—the belief in the freedom and rights of the individual—has repeatedly gained momentum in its history. And even if today's successes of liberalism are celebrated, these triumphs could paradoxically be its own downfall. Since its beginnings during the Enlightenment, liberalism has consistently fought against the shadows of totalitarianism. Today, however, the fabric of liberalism is strained. The attempted assignment of a fixed political theory meets the dynamics of our time and also the attempted taming and absolutization of "the economy." It seems to me that—ironically—the unchecked progress and freedom that have been brought to us in Western regions of prosperity may erode our social bonds and the common good. In the past, imbalance led to the collapse of the Eastern Bloc in 1990.

Today, liberal democracy faces similar challenges. It must defend and justify the path but how? What is forward, and what is backward? In the Viking Code, the Law of Jante represents something like grounding and community spirit, but it does not aim for complete transcendence. Rather, the awareness of community involvement can bring about a new understanding of team spirit in democracy and politics—and thus promote societal progress.

And here could lie a fascinating parallel: while the basic ideas of liberalism have not drastically changed, our world has changed, particularly in terms of technology. Often we throw around terms like "revolution," but behind it might only be the development of older themes. Essentially, society seeks a balance. In a society fluctuating between action and exhaustion, the question arises whether freedom can lead to less freedom.

What does that mean?

If our democracies do not adapt quickly enough to the technological age, division and lack of vision are the consequences. As in the description of finite and infinite games, politics in the form of democracy has a finite game: elections. But at its core, governing and navigating must have a creative component of infinity to create a stable world.

In stable times, populist tendencies can be managed. But in turbulent times, the societal fabric might tear. It's not just about the economy; it's about recognition and dignity. Everyone now has a powerful tool—the smartphone as a symbol of a connected world—to initiate change. Yet although revolutions like the Arab Spring, led by Internet activist Wael Ghonim, who knew how to use the digital network, seemed promising, they often wavered and stalled, underscoring the fragility of such movements. In the absolute pursuit of upheaval, they lack the integrative aspect, as we find in playing. By uncompromisingly rejecting the existing, its potential—or the power—for shaping the desired outcome is lost. Precisely that strength, which according to

Nassim Nicholas Taleb, leads to antifragility and thus opens the perspective for the infinite, for staying in the game, is lost.

In an age where a universal "model" to follow is missing, it seems as if the economic system is on the brink. Yet history suggests that revolutions may not be the inevitable outcome.

So, where do we stand? With liberty, equality, and fraternity in mind, we find our current society self-exploiting. We are both master and slave, driver and driven. Against whom do we then revolt in this self-imposed duality?

We find ourselves in a complex dance, attempting to balance progress with conservation, individualism with community, and freedom with responsibility. Perhaps the true face of the revolution today is not one of barricades and turmoil but one of introspection, self-reflection, and the eternal pursuit of a dynamic balance.

Yet the essence of democracy is its evolution, a living organism of constantly recurring ambition for progress. It is not static; it's about change and growth, lived also as playful ease. This perspective implies that democracy is constantly emerging, becoming. Labeling democracy—whether liberal, representative, or radical—might limit its essence. Democracy is not just about organizational structures; it's a promise, an ideal that is always in motion and always results from a collective approach—a common "dugnad," if you will—as the basis of an interdependent and desirable future.

True democracy, when claimed as absolute, contradicts its promise of freedom. Absolute freedom is an illusion, for in its absoluteness, it can restrict freedom. Democracy is therefore a delicate, infinite striving for dynamic balance, a bridge between what is and what could be.

What is our challenge then? To rethink the essence of freedom within our existing democratic framework. To actively shape a modern liberalism, receptive to global shifts—whether societal, technological, or environmental. To do this, we must free ourselves from established paradigms and let go of the world as we see it. We need vision and also utopia, but progress occurs in the next step, in action. The heroism in change lies in the action itself. We are Handlungshelden (heroes of action), where the path and the associated progress bring about the great change we recognize through fame, honor, and gold, but only understand in retrospect—as the path of infinite progress.

Educational, health, and financial institutions underestimate the forces of change that are already in full swing. What is understood as the task of the state is already being challenged today. Even the democratic models with their political parties seem not to provide the answers. Does this then lead to restoration?

The Revolt of the Rebellious Mayors

In a time when trust in the state is dwindling and state services fail to meet citizen expectations, the question arises: What will follow?

Historically, rebellions have also led to power takeovers and realignments. In our modern era, with technologically and militarily centralized structures, such a revolt seems hardly possible. Therefore, a realignment appears as an attractive alternative.

In our globalized world, local belonging, whether in a village, a city, a region, or a community of interest, plays a significant role. Challenges and opportunities are distributed differently everywhere, and more and more regional initiatives are emerging. Sometimes citizens take over tasks that were once the responsibility of the state.

In 2019, I wrote about a revolt of rebellious mayors, which was later slowed down by a global pandemic and the outbreak of a war in Europe. Since 2021, under the motto "Democracy Strikes Back," the think tank Innovation of Politics Institute has been bringing together mayors of various cities annually to discuss local challenges and joint projects. The project Mayors of Europe promotes cross-border cooperation, and the World Mayor of 2021, Peter Kurz from the German city of Mannheim, was invited to the G7 Summit to share his visions as a representative of the "rebellious mayors."

At global fairs like the Expo Berlin or the World Mobile Congress, cities and countries present their solutions for tomorrow's world. Not Germany, but the federal state of Baden-Württemberg provides global expertise for digital security technology to other states. Not Germany, but Heilbronn, led by entrepreneur Dieter Schwarz, takes the reins into its own hands and takes on the fight against American giants in terms of AI. And local politics follows suit, strengthening local identity and belonging and expanding design possibilities.

In this new landscape, where states and nations stay behind the scenes, interest groups and digital villages emerge, collaborating across borders and taking implementation into their own hands. Cities and federal states, led by unconventional mayors, bypass national guidelines, form cross-border alliances, and invigorate local identities. The state can often contribute only one thing: financial support—as long as the funds last.

When the Young Leave, We Will Look Old: Is This the End of Nation-states?

In the heart of America, enthusiastic Donald Trump supporters still hold up signs saying, "Take America back." These seemingly simple words, however, conceal a deep meaning and raise the question: What does it mean to reclaim a country, and from whom do we want it back? Progressive goals are indeed at the forefront, but they compete with resentments, and often negativity prevails.

Our era is marked by the attempt to define absolute opposition. This is not about standing for something, but against the existing. It's not just the challenge of a changed identity against which the nation-state has to fight. When citizens look for alternatives and think not only locally but globally, we are on a new path.

We are in fact on track in the next 10 years to experience a new country that will not be found on any map because its physical regions are scattered all over the world and it exists only as a network state. Equipped with its own digital passport, it will enable worldwide travel through new agreements. The criteria of a digital identity and belonging are being conceived today by emerging tech start-ups and could offer identity as a service through a "best-off" in terms of legislation, tax regulations, security, education, and fiscal policy, providing more value than any current national citizenship when it comes to pension insurance, health insurance, and all social services. Sondre Rasch, whom we met at the beginning of this chapter, represents just one of many start-ups already developing the products, services, and infrastructures of such citizenship.

When young, talented people migrate to the network state of digitization and flexibility, the traditional systems seem outdated. In most countries, systems are designed so that enough young, qualified people must pay into the system in order to finance future generations. We are talking about societal contributors who enable the welfare state through their above-average commitment and contributions. Should this not happen, states suddenly find themselves forced to advertise for people. If the finite game is then played, and the preparation for this competition has not been made, the outcome and existence of nation-states are not only uncertain but substantially threatened. Father State is now faced with the challenge of developing a high-performance culture rooted in values that can assert themselves in local and global competition.

We can already see what this looks like locally. The idyllic Swiss village of Albinen in the heart of the Alps offers significant financial support to those who settle there for more than 10 years. The municipal council put it succinctly in its written initiative: "With the departure of young people, the life in the village is also questioned for older citizens." The main goal was therefore to attract young people and families. But the people of Albinen quickly recognized the main problem with the departure: economic difficulties. Hence, this community initiative was launched.

As decided and approved by the municipality, the village pays a one-time housing subsidy to those willing to build or buy: US$27,500 for singles, US$55,000 for couples, and an additional $US11,000 for each child. For singles, the contribution increases by US$27,500 if a couple's household is formed within 10 years of moving in. In southern Italy's Calabria, new residents are paid premiums of US$30,000, which must be invested in starting a business.

The convergence of local identity and global dependencies challenges our notions of governance and representation. Could this be the future of governance?

Legislation could, in a sense, be viewed as arbitrarily adaptable "open source." Thus, "best of" global laws could be transferred to digital, parallel societies. With current technology, such a project is no longer unthinkable. Nowadays, everyone is connected, and thanks to AI and easy access, maybe just a pizza meeting and a weekend would be enough to start such an endeavor.

In this field of tension, new, decentralized offerings are emerging from such small "pizza teams," which offer agility and creativity to rival national structures. With DAOs—decentralized autonomous organizations—and their technological capabilities of Web 3.0, we are already experiencing the first parallel societies in action today. Technological interest groups and network states could even make entire nation-states obsolete.

Does this sound like utopia?

You think it won't come to this because the existing power structures will resist?

The current state of affairs alone may be surprising to many.

On October 30, 2023, more than 1,000 enthusiasts of the network state gather for a grand "class reunion" at the Taets Art and Event Park in Amsterdam. This event is organized by Balaji Srinivasan, an American serial entrepreneur, investor, and author of the book *The Network State: How to Start a New Country*. This conference is aimed at people interested in founding, funding, and building new communities and parallel societies.

The topics include start-up societies, network states, digital nomadism, competitive forms of government, legalization of innovations, and the development of alternative living arrangements. Speakers include leading figures from the tech scene driving this movement, including Glenn Greenwald, Vitalik Buterin, Anatoly Yakovenko, Garry Tan, the Winklevoss brothers, and Tyler Cowen. Behind the entrepreneurs presenting projects on stage are some of the most prominent investors from the technology sector, such as Elon Musk, Marc Andreessen, and Peter Thiel. It's about technology, but also about physical living concepts. Land plots and islands have already been purchased to build their own cities and residential areas for new interest groups. More acquisitions are to follow quickly. All participants seem to be in a hurry, yet present and decelerated in the matter.

On stage, the current projects are presented in rapid succession that day. Digital communities jointly finance resources to enable autonomous cities and states. The ideas in Srinivasan's book are inspired by the work of economist Albert O. Hirschman, who saw two fundamental ways for reform: voice (change the system from within) and exit (leave the system and build something new). While we consider voice as a local design tool today, exit for digital nomads is the ascent into a global network state: a highly organized online community that finances land, real estate, and properties worldwide and ultimately gains diplomatic recognition from existing states—if only because they can make their own offer more attractive through "bilateral" cooperation. Still, our imagination of the network state and local rebellions fails against our self-evident facts. And that's precisely why it's a risk for nation-states. Because we don't know the advantages and options—we don't understand what people want.

The network state functions like its own social network with moral innovation, a sense of national consciousness—a patriotism—and often a recognized founder, visionary, or leader who, however, has no claim to power over the creative force. The network state has the ability to act collectively, promotes a personal level of civility, has an integrated digital currency, and has a consensus-based government limited by social "smart contracts." In digital nomadism, there is an attractive selection of community-financed physical territories, a virtual capital, and an on-chain census—a true digital democracy.

It is entirely conceivable that existing regions within today's nation-states could take such a path. Catalonia in Spain is an example, or maybe Bavaria. And the question is not far off: When will the first federal state in the United States decide to leave—"Make America States Again"? A rebranding of Texas to "Tech-CaaS" (Technology Civilization as a Service) could soon be practically just a click away. Looking at the developments, we quickly realize that the development of decentralization is not a technological battle. The laws legalizing marijuana, gun laws, the abortion issue—these are all big social issues where the states have partly sued the central government and implemented their own laws.

I personally believe that this is closer than we can imagine today. If you think this is fantasy, distant future, or fiction, then at least let's think together about how Khaby Lame might live in 5 to 10 years.

You don't know Khaby Lame?

Admittedly, I had no idea either. Khaby Lame has 81 million followers on Instagram, almost equivalent to the population of

Germany. But that's just on Instagram. On TikTok, he has 160 million followers. Lame is only 23 years old.

He is known for his humorous short videos in which he makes fun of so-called life hacks and shows simpler, more obvious solutions in everyday life. Since August 2022, Lame is an Italian citizen, but the world is his stage. What happens to his followers if he moves to a new network state? How many would follow him? Maybe 10%? That would be about 30 million people with further growth of his reach. Today they are children and teenagers, tomorrow mature citizens who learn through enlightenment why the state does not provide certain services and why life could be simpler and better elsewhere. We cannot yet estimate the implications of this radiance and power. Except for superstars like Cristiano Ronaldo or Selena Gomez, we have only seen the beginning of how this will influence our society. Would 14% of Ronaldo's fans move with him to a hypothetical "Ronaldoania"? With more than 600 million followers, that would be a country bigger than Germany—with its own economy, industry, and purchasing power.

When influencers start founding start-up societies, the state could come under pressure. "Competition invigorates business," as the saying goes. Could this soon become a reality for citizenships as well? What can the state then offer? Represented by the digital "network union," partnerships and framework agreements are negotiated similar to those in the European Free Trade Association/European Economic Area. Offline in the physical world, trust is built; online, clarity and transparency reign. Digital currencies and "smart contracts" could make bureaucracy and middlemen, with their risks of corruption and exploitation, redundant.

At the Amsterdam meeting of network state enthusiasts, Srinivasan did not invite dreamers. On stage, existing interest communities with nearly 100,000 members are presented, which could function like flourishing states today.

One of the speakers on stage is Sondre Rasch.

Inspired by David Deutsch's *The Beginning of Infinity: Explanations That Transform the World* and the ideas of Karl Popper—that people are allowed to make mistakes, progress is always possible, and "better problems" can arise from problems—Rasch presents his mantra and his new company: Plumia.

Plumia is a provider in the ecosystem of network states and offers its own type of citizenship: "Citizenship as a Service." Which state can offer the best tailor-made package? This vision of citizenship for digital nomads is the core concept of Plumia.

The first stage for the network state was the conception and development of infrastructure projects, including basic technologies. The network state also needs a global social safety net, pension systems, healthcare, offers for people with disabilities, regulations for parental leave, and an institution for unemployment. The next step is the development of a global passport, a sort of "super passport" that is valid everywhere. This could be a type of Schengen visa for digital nomads.

Despite all the visions and future orientation, Sondre Rasch's explanations show how deeply rooted the understanding of the Viking Code is in Norwegian culture: he draws a parallel to Norse mythology. He describes how the old giant—a symbol for the state apparatus—is now disassembled and from it new, global offers emerge as attractive alternatives.

In Norse mythology, the giant Ymir is dismembered after his death by the gods Odin, Vili, and Vé to create the world. Ymir, the primeval giant and ancestor of the giants (Jotun), plays a central role in the creation story as it is transmitted in the Edda. From Ymir's body parts, the world was formed: his flesh became the earth, his blood the seas, his bones the mountains, his teeth and jawbones formed rocks and stones, his skull became the sky, held at the four corners by dwarves, and from his eyebrows came Midgard, the world of humans.

The network state initiative aims at nothing less than a new world order, based on the disassembled parts of the metaphorical "great giant." Sondre Rasch, a key figure in this process, knows the state apparatus from his own experience. As a former political advisor to the Norwegian government, he is familiar with the bureaucratic hurdles and burdens. The fact that even someone like him leaves Norway's solid social network—one of the world's most stable and secure states—with criticism of its lack of speed, indicates that even tech pioneers and designers in Germany might consider engaging in other areas.

Land as a vision of progress, a new state on the Internet, a second citizenship—is this utopia? Plumia already has 30,000 paying members today and generates an annual revenue of more than 25 million euros. And that's just the beginning.

Such a world will emerge. The question is, how do we deal with it? Should we resist it or welcome it as innovation and progress and actively co-create it? Personally, I would like to acquire land near Görlitz, raise a billion in capital, and build a new city there for 10,000 residents.

Why? Because this is precisely the type of "visionary" ideas that today's generation of designers is grappling with. They are not armed with weapons or demonstrations to overthrow the government, but with capital and technology to build the world of tomorrow. We are facing the greatest upheavals in human history regarding how we organize and live. In this redesign, commitment and values will play an important role.

How can the Viking Code accompany us on this journey?

The Viking Code in Organized Human Life

I believe that openness is now required to shape a rational, global society. This should define itself not only politically but also ecologically, technologically, and humanly.

Leadership must be a driving force for design and change and should not just mean a pursuit of power. A thriving democracy uses power to shape, activate, and introduce new things, not just to preserve our societal values but also to strengthen the humane. We should not become passive players but active architects of change. True leaders are characterized by acting with integrity even when they are unobserved. The Achilles' heel here is not technology, but our perception and understanding.

However, complacency remains our greatest challenge. Negativity, divisive politics, and insular thinking stand in the way of global harmony. Isn't it necessary today to look beyond the finite game—beyond short-term interests—and adopt a far-reaching worldview? The true value of a system lies in its ability to evolve and change.

A deep commitment is essential. Can we create an environment where different opinions are not only tolerated but also understood? Europe, with its rich artistic and cultural heritage, provides a suitable model for this. To truly enjoy personal freedoms, we need a collective "dugnad." It starts with a clear understanding of the world and our role in it. Such togetherness may seem distant, but cross-border network initiatives create forms of cooperation that offer hope. Even on a small scale, we can achieve a lot. The beginning of such an embellishment of our world lies in conversation with neighbors and in building community relationships.

The US Declaration of Independence enshrines the pursuit of individual happiness. Today, we need a new collective guiding principle. A *Declaration of Interdependence*—mutual dependency—would be a start that could initially be instigated by the United Nations, an institution of the old model, as a kind of starting shot and commitment to transformation. It's about setting the course for a world we can leave to our children and grandchildren with pride.

The Viking Code also praises the virtues of positivity. This does not mean blind optimism but a focused, constructive perspective that welcomes challenges as opportunities for growth. Today, in an era where the fundamental ideals of liberalism are being questioned, we are at a turning point. Populist movements and rifts in centralized politics show the need for a more inclusive form of liberalism. Europe stands at a crossroads, grappling with economic inequalities and a lack of common ideals. Yet the philosophy of the Viking Code could help shape a more harmonious future—one with "better problems."

The Viking Code represents a balanced pursuit of power, offering a different paradigm. It does not reject ambition but combines it with values and virtues. It advocates using inner drive for the common good. Instead of emphasizing only individual success, it promotes collective achievements and creates an environment where high performance is equated with ethical action.

The Viking Code provides concrete guidance. It recognizes the pitfalls of uncontrolled ambition and offers a harmonious alternative. In this ethos, success becomes a collective celebration, and each achievement contributes to a collective crescendo. It is a model of progress, something dynamic and alive, an embellishment of European values.

If the Viking Code provides insights for organized human life, it especially emphasizes the importance of learning—and particularly, how we learn. To realign or refine organized human life and stimulate a global educational renaissance that promotes a mindset focused not on the "what" but the "how" of thinking, we need a stable operating system.

This dynamic understanding applies not only to democracy. A creative force must also shape the operating system—the economy. I advocate for an "emerging" (humane) capitalism that has not yet existed. The idea of Jacques Derrida's "coming democracy" and my concept of an "emerging capitalism" remind us never to be complacent in our pursuit of harmony. There is always room for improvement and change. This is both a critique of existing democratic systems and a call to continuously strive for more justice, equality, and freedom.

In the next and final chapter, we explore this possibility. We examine how the once scorned and ridiculed capitalism of limitation can evolve into an infinite approach of humane capitalism: the "Quantum Economy."

10

Operating System: The Viking Code and the Economy

ON A COOL March day in early 2023, a young woman with braids stands in front of the Ministry of Petroleum and Energy in Norway. She meets with a group of like-minded people. Each breath in the icy air is a sign of her determination. However, her protest is not against the usual suspects, the real or supposed fossil resource lobby, but against the wind parks in Fosen.

To the casual observer, Fosen might just seem like a windy peninsula in central Norway. But in fact, it is one of Norway's windier places, with the potential to become a green energy hub. Here, at the Trondheimsfjord, Norway is realizing an ambitious project: the complete transition to renewable energy.

But the climate activists, led by Greta Thunberg, want the turbines already installed on the peninsula—symbols of hope for many—removed. An environmental activist against green energy—how does that fit together?

The answer lies with the Sami, an indigenous people of Scandinavia. Their reindeer, which play a central role in their way of life, are displaced by the wind turbines. According to a court ruling in 2021, the rights of the Sami are violated by these wind parks. Greta Thunberg's message is clear: green energy, yes—but not at any cost.

While intense debates on climate and international law are held in Norway, young activists in the bustling streets of an Indian metropolis advocate for education as a means to fight poverty. At the same time, economists in the glass towers of Frankfurt and New York are designing visions of a future, prosperous world. Everywhere, discussions are taking place on the diverse aspects of what we understand by "sustainability." We are dealing with an interplay that is highly characterized by interdependencies. The issue of "sustainability" can often be visualized as a three-legged tripod that keeps our world stable:

- The first leg, **ecological sustainability**, symbolizes the world as a vulnerable organism. It calls for fewer toxins in our atmosphere, a respect for what we consume, and a striving to not only protect but celebrate biodiversity.
- The second leg, **social sustainability**, illustrates the social fabric that surrounds us. It points to a future where each of us, regardless of our background, has an equal, if not better, chance to prosper.
- And the third leg, **economic sustainability**, is not just an acronym for profit. It calls for creating wealth without neglecting people and the planet.

If just one of these legs wobbles, the entire tripod can collapse. Our economy, often perceived as heartless and sterile, is the subtle binding agent that links everything together. I refer to the economy as the operating system of our society. We come closer to the goal of an ecological and social market economy when the economy is stable or functioning and allows for social redistribution. It becomes ecological when it is possible to create a symbiosis of ecology and economy. I am convinced that if we succeed in creating incentives for behavior changes and making business models for circular economy and regenerative approaches profitable, then we will realize that progress is our only true option and we do not find all answers in the existing, but in the unknown new possibilities.

So, are we talking about a technological and economic utopia? Of course, it's not that simple.

I am also firmly convinced that we in Western affluent regions—not only in terms of environment and climate—can and must significantly reduce our consumption and use (re-duce), and I am for regulations and limitations that enable reusability (re-use).

However, for me it is all about moving beyond sustainability. I believe that positive progression through technological development and new approaches are the bigger lever to create a stable foundation—a tripod—for our world (re-think).

The Quantum Economy: A New Paradigm

In the shadow of World War II, Ludwig Erhard, serving under German Chancellor Konrad Adenauer, formulated the passionate promise of "Prosperity for All." It was not just an empty political promise; this assurance represented the supporting framework of the German economic strategy. His vision of an inclusive social market economy made the German "economic miracle" a reality and set in motion a capitalism model that brought about remarkable achievements like peace, increased life expectancy, and the reduction of extreme poverty.

However, weaknesses of this model have become apparent over time. What is demanded of us today? An economic model that embodies socio-ecological principles and combines human welfare with economic prosperity. Too often, our earth, our home and its inhabitants, have been sidelined in favor of relentless profit-seeking.

In 1972, the Club of Rome presented its groundbreaking work: the Limits to Growth. Half a century later, its central message echoes louder than ever: The deeply intertwined treasures of our planet—this global, natural network that unites us all—might not withstand the current rates of economic and population expansion, despite all our technological advances.

Capitalism, as we seemingly know it well, has proven its robustness as a pillar of progress. But, as the Dalai Lama aptly noted, albeit paraphrased: "Capitalism is a working model, but it needs compassion." Perhaps, then, the solution is not to discard capitalism, but to refine and optimize it? A finer patchwork model, at whose heart humanity is woven.

And here we stand on the threshold of significant evolution. It's not enough to merely add modern concepts like "impact investments" or "social business." Instead, imagine a comprehensive update of our societal operating system, a revolutionary redesign at the heart of our understanding of economics. I call this new paradigm "Quantum Economy."

The Quantum Economy radically differs in its approach from the understanding of conventional economics. In classical physics, theories are based on fixed, immutable laws. Everything is predictable. Quantum mechanics, on the other hand, shows us a world of probabilities, uncertainties, entanglements, and interconnected relationships.

The question we face is this: What happens when we apply this quantum mechanical framework to our economy?

Understanding Quantum Economy, we recognize that nothing is isolated. Everything affects everything. An economic decision in Europe can impact a small village in Asia. An oil price increase or, as recently, a war in Europe affects food security in Africa. The missing toilet paper amid the COVID-19 pandemic shows us the interplay of supply chains. These insights open up the possibility of thinking beyond linear causalities and developing a deep understanding of the interactions and diverse dependencies that exist in our globalized world. And it is this growing perception that leads us to reflect dynamically and infinitely on the economy and to refine the capitalist system—to give it an upgrade—and thus understand the economy as something in the making.

Furthermore, it reminds us that in a connected world, improving one problem often has the potential to improve many other problems simultaneously. Just as in quantum physics a particle can be in a state of "entanglement" with another particle, in the Quantum Economy, social, ecological, and economic solutions can come into play simultaneously if we choose the right approach.

Imagine a world where companies not only make profits but also contribute to solving global challenges—whether it's climate change, social injustice, or education. A company in this new economy considers not only the interests of its shareholders but also those of its community, environment, and even future generations. Sounds familiar? Isn't this the image we got to know in the Viking Code?

The Quantum Economy is a vision that goes beyond the existing paradigm—a model that tries to combine the best of capitalism and compassion, technology and humanity, and leads us to a more sustainable, fairer, and prosperous future.

It's not only our responsibility but also our opportunity to take this path. Because in times when the challenges are as complex as never before, we need new approaches and models that not only help us survive but also grow and better understand our problems.

The Quantum Economy pulsates with dynamics and captures the paradoxes of our time. Inspired by quantum physics, it subjects our established economic notions to scrutiny, just as once the quantum concepts shook the conventional physics. A theoretical tremor back then that shattered our view of reality is now, a century later, finding concrete applications. Just as quantum mechanics revolutionized our understanding of matter, the Quantum Economy questions our economic beliefs and the complex fabric of our existence. It's a call to break binary thinking patterns and broaden the horizon of our rigid economic concepts. The unification of rational compassion and capitalism presupposes a profound understanding of current challenges, intricacies, and dynamics.

An economy viewed as a closed system, based on results, victories and defeats, and permeated by a finite perspective—homeostasis—is ultimately a dead system.

However, the Quantum Economy does not strive for finite victory or defeat; it rather embodies an infinite vision of economics. In a Quantum Economy, it's not about winning or losing, but playing as long as possible. It celebrates the endeavor of companies and organizations to stay in the game as long as possible—to exist in the limitless game. A Quantum Economy is a dynamic system—homeodynamic—that integrates humans and the planet into its basic fabric and reinterprets the essence of capitalism. This system introduces a "new art of entrepreneurship," where humans and the planet are not peripheral issues but the foundation.

At the heart of the Quantum Economy and its "infinite organizations" pulses a central motif: the mensch. This word—firmly rooted in the German language—denotes a proactive, forward-looking being, symbolizing our unstoppable force to discover ever better problems and shape progress in a positive sense.

The vital economic perspective of the Quantum Economy draws its essence from the thoughts of theologian James P. Carse in *Finite and Infinite Games: The Opportunities of Life*. Carse designed an impressive dichotomy: the finite and the infinite game. Think of a chess game—clear rules, protagonists, and ultimately a champion. That embodies the finite game. But what if there was no fixed end point? If the main goal was simply continuation, constant blossoming, and adapting? That's exactly what the infinite game embodies. Simon Sinek, in his works, also builds on Carse's ideas and illuminates how they can be transferred to leadership and corporate structure in *The Infinite Game—Strategies for Lasting Success.*

When I formulated the concept of the Quantum Economy 5 years ago, it was mainly based on a vision and an intuition. Now, a few years later, I already see the first contours of this economic model flourishing, with contemporary Vikings paving the way. They carry the Viking Code with them in their baggage.

Viking Code Meets Quantum Economy: The "Better Problem"

Is flying bad? How can we create a climate-friendly future? To begin, here's a thought that might provoke many: What if the answer lies not in flying less, but more? Wouldn't the promise of greater returns not only be the reward but also the catalyst for groundbreaking research and development?

Such questions divide and provoke. Climate activists are clear in a world of absolute answers and knowledge: "I know flying is harmful, so we must reduce it." Capitalists, however, disagree.

But what if I rephrase the question: What if we could create a world where airplanes act like giant vacuum cleaners, sucking CO_2 from the air and converting it into energy? A world where flying not only reduces emissions but actively "repairs" our atmosphere according to scientific findings?

If that were possible, surely more would agree.

Does such a scenario sound too far-fetched?

From a scientific and physics-derived point of view, there are still some challenges to implementing such a vision. Meanwhile, some airlines have been investing in carbon capturing, sequestration, and storage of carbon dioxide for years now—and it's a thriving billion-dollar industry. Oil companies have already made their investments. Research with alternative fuels like waste, frying oil, or various forms of green energy is also being conducted and making progress.

This is just the beginning.

However, traveling in the air is a complex problem with multiple dimensions to consider. Therefore, it serves as a good example of the challenges of our time. Here's the issue: A disjointed view of airplane emissions is a one-dimensional representation. Air travel, however, has many dimensions.

Let's start with a simple observation: Take a moment and think about a busy airport you recently visited. Even without the holiday rush, the terminal is full, the runways are occupied. Environmentally conscious people, who preach sustainability, need their annual vacation or retreat into nature. The lure of an occasional sabbatical on a distant beach or a yoga retreat in Bali is hard to resist and is part of our "maturation process" as human beings. It's not just business travelers or adventure seekers. In other words: Is it realistic to expect that we will fly less enough? At this point, I want to emphasize that we in Western affluent regions can and must reduce and limit. But even here, I am convinced that this doesn't happen through coercion, but rather through motivation—through attractive alternatives and incentives or through changed education that can influence people's behavior over generations through a different understanding of values. Regulations and bans fall far short for a realistic future scenario.

The second question, which may also disturb many environmentalists, is this: Isn't flying—or effective air travel—one of the great inventions that have enabled us humans to live better together, and thus an essential part of an interdependent global community? Should we isolate ourselves more and live more locally? Or are traveling and collaboration the only realistic scenario in a highly digitalized and connected world to broaden our horizons and work together on conflicts?

As already described in the chapter on politics, I clearly advocate for both: we need a stronger local identity and belonging, but also a stronger global connectedness and striving for a global community. Do we believe that a life in separate cultures and countries with different interests can exist in a digitally connected global society? We quickly realize that the problem we are dealing with here is the technology that enables flying, not flying itself.

This brings us to another consideration regarding market development and the underlying forces of change. In other words, what options are realistic to bring about an improvement of the problem in the medium and long term? The problem may not be traveling by plane, but the technology with which we travel. The challenge with energy and fuel is not a lack of options, but a storage and distribution problem—the sun alone offers "infinite possibilities." Yet, we expect the aviation industry to reduce and limit. From a human perspective and considering the needs (i.e., demand), there is indeed the legitimate question of whether "braking" is even an option.

Because from today's approximately four billion passengers, projections say there will be eight billion by 2050. Now such numbers may overshoot the target and be based on simple errors in assumptions, but if we look at the numbers from which we could draw conclusions, we might come to a similar result: Western affluent countries have an aging population that is capital-strong and doesn't want to work. What will they do? Fly.

Moreover, we look at a continent like Africa with a population that is generating more and more wealth. Isn't it foreseeable that with a growing middle class, the desire for air travel will also increase? The skies over Nairobi, Lagos, and Johannesburg will soon be busier than ever. If the predictions are accurate and Africa's population swells from today's one and a half billion to an incredible four billion in just a few decades, how can we reconcile this with our vision of a sustainable future?

The question I ask myself is whether our current strategies such as promoting the circular economy or resource efficiency will be sufficient?

Looking at emerging countries, the development seems clear. New airlines will emerge, old ones will expand. The logos will be removed from the old planes in the thriving markets, and the fleets will be slowly modernized with newer and better aircraft. At the same time, in the emerging markets, the old planes get a second life with new logos and colors, which only exacerbates the problem.

A slow deceleration, regulation, and limitation will probably lead to a slowdown in technological progress, as the market will no longer be attractive for investments. If we then try to meet the increasing demand with old technologies, it's more like dying a slow death.

If the increasing demand for global mobility should no longer burden our planet, what impulses could also come from new companies to innovate faster, invest more, and find answers that haven't even been considered yet?

Capitalism Upgrade: The Story of Creative Destruction

Crises and limitations are efficacious but only to a certain degree, and progress is slow. Instead, the focus should be on enabling "better problems"—better products and incentives for behavioral changes. If the goal is to reduce volume, price is just one tool. However, alternative approaches can be more effective. Someone who wants to fly but can't afford it will still try to find the means. If offered an attractive deal or product, the change in behavior is driven by intrinsic motivation. That's real transformation. Thus, supporting pioneers and tech companies willing to innovate is essential.

What if the challenges we face are actually catalysts for change? Every major leap in history was preceded by seemingly insurmountable obstacles. Less than 50 years separated the Wright brothers' first flight on a sandy strip in North Carolina from the harnessing of quantum mechanics and the first atomic bombs. Today, jumbo jets crisscross the skies, shrinking our vast world into a global village. The history of aviation is a testament to human ingenuity. How far can we dream? How bold can our ambitions be? Perhaps a different perspective on problems is needed.

Aviation is just a simplified example of how problems and solutions can be handled today. Restrictions and regulations can hinder a new culture of performance and entrepreneurship. We search for answers and solutions. But what if we shift our focus?

When the first Internet browsers appeared, they were text-based, and the network connections were slow. It would have made sense to optimize HTML into a more technical language. Instead, Netscape's founders decided to support images. The appeal of seeing pictures created new possibilities and incentives for innovation and network expansion. Where would we be today if Netflix hadn't shifted from DVD rentals to streaming, despite slow Internet connections? Making streaming attractive led to better infrastructure. We can address many societal challenges similarly today. For instance, a research team at Cambridge University has developed a machine that uses solar energy to convert CO_2 and plastic waste into fuel. The Manta sailboat collects plastic from the oceans and converts it into energy.

How can we create incentives for faster change? Just 9 months after Russia's invasion of Ukraine, Germany managed to decouple from Russian gas. Do we always need crises to prompt action? I believe there must be other ways.

Here's a thesis: In 10 to 15 years, the marginal costs for energy will plummet toward zero, and we'll witness a transformative change akin to today's AI revolution. We will soon have almost unlimited, low-cost energy. Initially, this will lead to insights that prompt many "experts" to look back in order to look forward. Scarcity in transistors and pressure on rare materials will increase, followed by a shortage of power in watts. As transport and heating electrify and technology like AI expands, electricity demand will double or triple in the next 3 to 4 years. This will create a huge demand for batteries so that energy needs don't always have to be met in real time. Increased investments and technological advancements, along with the development of new energy forms like hydrogen, will enhance profitability and intensify cost pressure as renewable energy becomes viable.

If this thesis is correct, companies that align their business models and invest accordingly today will succeed in the coming decades.

Now, our flight example takes on a new dimension. If our bet on the future is accurate, and if the necessary facilities are built and ordered, we might unnecessarily prolong climate-damaging emissions. Imagine a world where powering a city or charging a car costs almost nothing. Sounds like a dream, right? But what if I told you this utopian marketplace is just around the corner? As technology evolves, it not only produces gadgets but also reshapes economic systems. The sun offers 10,000 times more power than we currently use. The challenge is not in generation but in capturing and distributing it. Our planet, with its winds, waters, and sunlight, is not just a home but a power plant waiting to be tapped.

This isn't about flying or energy, but understanding a paradigm shift in the economy—an upgrade of capitalism toward a circular, regenerative model. This is the Quantum Economy.

I foresee a future where the limitations we once complained about—in energy, in knowledge—become almost negligible. We've already seen the cost of acquiring knowledge plummet. If energy follows, then the approach to ecological issues becomes purely economic. Hyperefficiency will be the foundation of business survival. The key question for companies is this: How can we make money in the future when today's resource-intensive product becomes freely available tomorrow?

The future of sustainability isn't about charity or high ideals, reductionism or limitation; it's about profit. It's about how a company can survive in an infinite game. The goal is to stay in the game as long as possible. A company that doesn't prioritize resource efficiency will be sidelined and unprofitable. The path forward is to recognize that the next wave of business models will integrate economics and ecology. The future of the economy lies in profiting from preserving our world.

The year 2024 is as far from 1981 as 1938 was from 1981. What will our world look like in 2067? In the movie *2067*, Ethan (played by Kodi Smit-MchPhee) questions his ability to save the world: "You don't really think I can save the world, do you?" Every technological miracle, every disruptive creation begins as a dream. It seems utopian, almost fictional, until it suddenly becomes the world we live in. There's no reason it can't become reality. The real challenges lie in economics and technology. In other words, it's about investment and innovation. What kind of future do you anticipate?

The Infinite Organization: Prosperity for Posterity

When we look at the Quantum Economy as the operating system of our society, then the organizations that interact and run on the operating system are analogous to the apps. Users—the people—influence these organizations both from the inside and the outside.

This creates a complex, dynamic system of interdependencies, which represents, shapes, and enlivens the interplay of the economy in all its possibilities.

Today, most organizations in the economy behave like participants in a finite game. They breathlessly chase the next quarterly profit, market share increase, and immediate gratification of short-term goals. In doing so, they strongly focus on satisfying market needs. This dynamic often resembles a sporting competition, where it's about winning or losing. In times of crisis, these organizations react immediately and absolutely. If the quarterly goal fails, heads roll—regardless of whether the strategic direction is correct. In a fast-paced and complex market environment, short-term and absolute goals for ensuring measurability are increasingly narrow.

As complexity and speed increase, managers shorten their planning cycles and limit their environment to maintain control rather than exploring the potentials and opportunities of the changed environment. With increasing uncertainty, short-term goals come to the forefront, and the long-term vision falls behind.

This development is also observed in start-ups and young companies that quickly seek funding and rapid growth—growth for the sake of growth—until a high valuation is achieved that allows an IPO or another round of financing. To meet economic goals and obligations to markets or investors, the company is often sold to achieve finite goals both in the corporate context and in personal life. Everything is measurable and countable.

This finite view of organizations ultimately leads to the finiteness of the entire system itself due to increasing speed and complexity, similar to if one app on an operating system takes up all the resources, the system comes to a halt.

But amid this frantic race, new types of organizations are emerging that recognize that the art of doing business cannot be a finite game in the style of sports competitions, but an infinite game with a multitude of interconnected complexities. These organizations understand short-term changes as opportunities, where reactive behavior is part of long-term reflection. The infinite organizations are characterized above all by a lack of absolute definition. It consists of a recurring pursuit of progress, a dynamic understanding of short-term goals and long-term visions.

Looking at the success of the German economy, we encounter large family businesses that have pursued an infinite philosophy over generations. They have not only provided for the current generation but also taken responsibility to ensure that subsequent generations will be successful. I refer to the philosophy of these organizations as "prosterity"—their aim is prosperity for posterity, taking both the short term and the long term into account. They are characterized by a focus both on local and regional responsibility and on surviving in global competition.

These companies are infinite in their orientation due to their responsibility and family ties. World market leader Fischer Dübel met both the social aspect and societal responsibility when company founder Arthur Fischer developed Fischertechnik construction kits from his Christmas gift to the children of partners. From the dowel manufacturer grew a second business segment that covered both the playful and the educational. Today, Fischertechnik delivers toys and educational learning concepts around robotics and modern technology, builds its own construction robot that can dowel, and cracked the billion in sales for the first time in 2023.

Many hidden champions and family businesses deal with contradictions and show a high tolerance for ambiguity—they must create a basis for the existence of the family and at the same time ensure that they remain true to "prosterity."

In the 1980s and 1990s, the focus shifted to short-term optimization and maximization. We witnessed the birth of the dot-com mentality and the glorification of shareholder value. A one-sided focus on optimization and short-term maximization in its extreme led to the finiteness and consequently to a collapse of the entire economic system. We now therefore recognize that an upgrade to our understanding and capitalistic model is needed.

What characterizes an infinite organization?

Infinite organizations are characterized by a high tolerance for ambiguity+ as they not only welcome contradictions, but they also love "the unknown." They welcome complexities and see crises and changes—i.e., the unknown—as opportunities for progress. For infinite organizations, surprise is an opportunity to find creativity in uncertainty. They do not maximize for short-term economic success but optimize for permanence and infinity.

Infinite organizations do not only serve economic goals and the sole fulfillment of shareholder expectations but consider all stakeholders. In their actions, ecology and economy merge into a harmonious interplay. Social responsibility and a deep understanding of culture and ecosystems are integral parts of their DNA. They utilize the possibilities of technology and scientific progress. They measure what is measurable and introduce metrics that consider culture and human well-being as well as the entire ecology.

As an analogy for the infinite organization, let's consider an example from sports. When an athlete is injured, it opens a new basis for progress. Long-term positive developments and the associated crises require a renewed focus on progress. Transferring this thinking to an organization, we speak of an infinite organization. And here the relevance of the Viking Code and the analogy to the modern Vikings becomes clear. These athletes master not only the finite games, they are experts in setting measurable goals within the infinite games. They recognize that playing itself is the basis for every finite victory.

In infinite organizations, managers with finite thinking are not trained, but rather "infinite leaders." These leaders know how to celebrate short-term successes—similar to athletes in competitions—but for them, the game does not end there. When a soccer player like Haaland scores goals and the game ends, it's just one stage of his sporting journey. The Viking Code teaches us that in the moment—the now—it's about achieving goals and winning victories, but the real success lies in continuous progress, in the journey and development. Athletes and leaders who follow the Viking Code understand that infinite progress—and thus the journey—is the basis for success. Qualitative input leads to accumulated output, from which progress can be derived.

Similar to the infinite progress mindset of a performance athlete who sees the journey as his goal and constantly strives for daily micro-ambitions, we can understand infinite organizations as communities whose members achieve their small daily progresses, which in sum lead to great success. The success of infinite organizations is often quiet, perhaps even inconspicuous. Here you will find no controlling, audible authority. In infinite organizations, management is part of the technology: tasks, overviews, and reports flow from the technology, while people act as leaders. They shape their own path, environment, and successes. They are on their individual journey and at the same time part of the collective. In infinite organizations, people come to learn and grow; it's about constant progress.

In the Quantum Economy, where economics and ecology are synergistic and a new generation of conscious young people is emerging, it is these infinite organizations that understand that true success is not measured only in profits but in the positive impact they have on the world. Such organizations see beyond the here and now. It's not just about being the best in the market but being the best for the world. Infinite organizations understand that in a rapidly changing world, success is a journey, not a destination.

The leaders, visionaries, and founders of these modern organizations are not caught in the familiar tug-of-war between work and life—the work-life balance. Instead, they dance to a different rhythm—the life-life balance—which can never be in balance. It's a delicate dance, not of perfect balance but of dynamic harmony. The shapers of the infinite organization are not looking for a single, defined purpose. They take on an infinite journey, not to a predetermined destination, but to an exciting journey into the unknown. The journey is the true art of doing business.

In this new paradigm, traditional definitions of management and leadership are being rewritten. Gone are the days of rigid structures. Now it's about dynamics and the active capability to navigate through the uncertainties of the global market while maintaining an unshakable core rooted in timeless principles.

Organizations face a profound realization: It's no longer just about beginning and end. It's about endurance, evolution, and flourishing. This holistic view changes the art of doing business.

The holistic perspective at the heart of the infinite organization is anchored in a robust ethos. Its design principles—*the cultural dimension*—reminiscent of the Viking Code, revolve around a willingness to learn and a pursuit of constant progress.

The infinite organization marks a change: from static "experts" and knowledge workers to dynamic "professional amateurs" who seek deeper insights and understanding. Inspired by the concept of "shoshin," the organization emphasizes not only learning but also the art of knowledge transfer.

In the ecosystem—*the external dimension*—of the infinite organization, a dynamic balance prevails among competition, coexistence, and shared values. These are oriented toward both immediate needs and long-term aspirations. Today, this means building a connected, decentralized intelligence, forming strong local and regional identities, and aligning with global dependencies. In doing so, the organization strives for a balance between stability and receptivity to change.

The backbone of the infinite organization is *the structural dimension*—the management. Here, effectiveness, efficiency, and technological prowess converge. The foundation of the organization's operational excellence is technology, which explores boundaries, explores new frontiers, and creates within defined parameters. Here, the infinite game is mastered through strategic clarity.

While today's management focuses on executing tasks perfectly with technology, the true essence of leadership—*the activating dimension*—focuses on recognizing and pursuing what really matters: fostering a culture of excellence rooted in core values and ensuring positive progress through action. This perspective attempts to define the place of humans in an ever-evolving technological landscape, to give meaning, and to steer life. With genuine leadership and trust, we move from a zero-sum game of absolute competition to a collaborative coexistence.

The concept of "infinity" is abstract, yet it is the foundation of the infinite organization.

Such organizations are shaped through proactive engagement with progress. This proactive self-awareness is not derived from textbooks but is rooted in a deep understanding that ignites genuine motivation. It is the embodiment of the values of the Viking Code that shapes the path of leaders and is anchored in the culture of the infinite organization.

To make this infinite mindset more tangible, let's think about the legacy of our grandparents. They spoke of hard work, sacrifice, and the dream of a better future. For them, progress was a necessity for survival in the present. Today, especially in affluent countries, there is a lack of urgency, even though it concerns the survival of humanity.

Our challenge today is to expand prosperity, free countless people from the clutches of poverty, and at the same time protect the well-being of future generations. The collective consciousness is undoubtedly aware of the impending challenges—headlines announce impending crises, discussions flare up about the latest scientific findings. But do these alarm signals truly serve as catalysts for change?

The demand of the hour is a newly rethought approach to activation—a clear call for a culture of high performance, deeply rooted in timeless values.

The infinite organization is aware of this. It harnesses the power of technology, not just as a tool but as an ally, to streamline, explore new territories, and drive forward. However, at its core, it serves the "human touch." It is the intuition, the spark of creativity, the compassion that a machine cannot imitate—at least not yet, as of today. In this organization, algorithms may set the course, but it is human values that set the compass. It's a symphony of high tech and high touch, striving playfully toward perfect harmony.

In a world where technology is ubiquitous, humans stand as equals to it. This dynamic equilibrium forms the foundation of infinite leadership. But what really defines a "mensch"? What are the characteristics of the infinite leader in the realm of the infinite organization? How is leadership shaped in the Quantum Economy?

In the complexity of modern leadership, infinite leaders stand out. They are not swayed by the fleeting highs and lows of the market or the short-lived applause of the crowd. While traditional leadership traits—vision, strategy, charisma—remain relevant, the Quantum Economy demands more. It calls for leaders with insatiable curiosity, an unshakeable commitment to learning, and a genuine desire to unleash the (human) potential in their environment. They play not just to win; they play to keep the game going indefinitely. For the infinite leader, it's not just about personal accolades or corporate milestones, but about creating positive impacts, nurturing ecosystems, and communicating narratives of progress that inspire future generations.

In this new era, leadership is no longer just a role or a title. It is a mindset, a philosophy, a way of life. It's about grasping the broader perspective, understanding that balancing work and life is really about every step we take—and that true balance is always in motion. As the world approaches an uncertain future, infinite leaders stand unwavering, showing the way forward with wisdom, grace, and unshakeable determination.

When I wrote about this back in 2018, the implication was not clear. Now inspired by the Viking Code, these leaders embody resilience. They understand that setbacks are merely stepping stones, that every challenge is an invitation to innovate, and that every failure is a hidden lesson. Infinite leaders remain steadfast, always ready to adapt and evolve. They embody a high tolerance for ambiguity and also the unknown, which I refer to as ambiguity+. The infinite leader understands the collective as a "dugnad" and contributes to the common good.

This is the allure of the infinite organization. It does not just function; it flourishes and draws vitality from the collective spirit of its members. It understands that the path to true excellence is not only marked by profits but also by a purpose. And as it sets its course in the complex world of economics, the Viking Code serves as its guiding star, leading it to a horizon where success and purpose are harmoniously intertwined.

Early Signs of the Quantum Economy

For nearly a decade, I have been searching for this dynamic equilibrium and a way to understand and describe infinite, humanly possible progress. I am still at the beginning of this search. However, I am convinced that focusing on finite solutions, answers, and positing absolutes is humanity's greatest limitation. It may even pose an existential threat, thus preventing humanity from confronting global challenges at their source. Understanding the Quantum Economy, then, lies not in statics or absolute answers, but in grasping the dynamic, based on our ability to accept infinite progress. Alongside many analogies to exponential technologies, the possibilities of quantum computers and their hybrid solutions, it is above all the philosophical understanding of quantum mechanics and an understanding of human growth that allows building a bridge between science and business, philosophy and economics, humanity and technology.

A century after the major breakthroughs in quantum theory, both its practical implications and its philosophical aspects are now in focus. A hundred years ago, it was philosophical thoughts and inspirations that created the theoretical basis of modern physics.

Danish physicist Niels Bohr, known for his rationality and as one of the pioneers of quantum mechanics, developed a unique way of thinking and ability to question established scientific theories and develop new concepts. His atomic model, introduced in 1913, revolutionized the understanding of atomic structure and was a milestone in the development of quantum theory. In addition to his scientific genius, Bohr was also known for his philosophical reflections. He was interested in the philosophical implications of quantum mechanics and made significant contributions to the debate on topics such as complementarity and the limits of knowledge.

Despite his individual achievements, he was also firmly convinced that a collaborative approach contributes to the common good and advances science. He worked with many other leading physicists of his time, including Albert Einstein, with whom he had famous debates about the interpretation of quantum mechanics. Albert Einstein, who in his later years suffered more from "philosophical troubles," also dealt with the implications of his theories and often discussed questions with philosophers like Bertrand Russell and others.

Werner Heisenberg, the father of the uncertainty principle, was also influenced by philosophical concepts and intensely engaged with Plato's writings. He was fascinated by questions about the nature of reality. Mathematician John von Neumann, who also made significant contributions to quantum mechanics, was active in philosophy and logic. His interest in the philosophy of mind and mathematics influenced his work in quantum physics.

These scientists and their engagement with philosophical questions show how closely quantum physics and philosophy are linked and how philosophical considerations have influenced the development of quantum physics.

Today, as we deal with a Quantum Economy, we are exploring not only the potential of technological progress but also philosophical contemplation. For me, philosophy is a thinking practice. As thinkers of *our* time, we have the opportunity to bring our thoughts to life thanks to economic and technological circumstances.

One of the best-known quantum physicists influenced by Buddhist ideas was Wolfgang Pauli, an Austrian physicist known for his work in quantum mechanics, particularly the so-called Pauli Exclusion Principle, which explains the structure of atoms by stating that two electrons in an atom cannot match in all quantum numbers. Pauli had a wide range of interests in philosophical and spiritual questions, including Buddhism.

He conducted a long-standing dialogue with the founder of analytical psychology, Carl Gustav Jung, who was heavily influenced by Eastern philosophies. Jung's writings and correspondence show that he was impressed by some aspects of Buddhism, particularly its views on the nature of reality and the limits of the human mind.

Erwin Schrödinger, the originator of one of the fundamental equations of quantum mechanics, named after him the Schrödinger equation, also dealt with Eastern philosophies, particularly Vedanta philosophy, an essential part of Hindu philosophy, which shares similarities with Buddhism. His famous thought experiment, "Schrödinger's Cat," for example, reflects a view that has similarities with the Buddhist concept of non-duality.

Questions about the nature of reality and the role of the observer in physics are today shifting from the theoretically charged towers of academia to the modern companies and icons of the Quantum Economy. Capital and technological possibilities will soon lure the brightest minds of science into the heart of capitalism. In the field of quantum technology, the race for top thinkers has long been underway, even if business models are not yet developed. Scientific progress and patent applications are increasingly coming from the corporate world.

When the first Nobel Prizes are awarded to teams in companies, or when technologies enable us to build things before an extended understanding of modern physics follows, we are facing an entirely new development in science. Only by trying out and building do we theoretically open up possibilities to reflect on the implications and our understanding.

And so, we already see today the first signs of a new economy. A new world that has never existed in this form before. It builds on our history but is just as shaped by its dynamics, unpredictability, and possibilities as by its foundation of predictability and statics. The future cannot be researched or studied. However, we humans have the ability to "future"—we can shape it. Apart from deterministic worldviews, simulation hypothesis, and other philosophical discourses on the nature of reality, we can influence our own lives.

My thoughts and theses in this book are based on hope, progress, and a decade of collaboration with leading quantum physicists and work with thought leaders in the fields of AI and exponential technologies. The technological implications of the next 10 years may seem like an existential threat to humanity, but at the same time, progress in technology and science allows us to create a better world—"better problems," not perfect, but more just, with less suffering, wars, and poverty, and a step toward an ecology that allows 10 billion people a desirable future. The exchange with numerous people from all over the world gives me confidence: we can do more; we can do it together.

Pioneers of the Blue and Green Economy

"Before we start, can you tell me how to properly pronounce your name?" A peculiar silence followed by embarrassed laughter.

"To be honest, I'm not sure myself, but I think you did quite well," Murshid M. Ali replies in a pronounced Stavanger dialect. He is a guest on a start-up podcast hosted by Christopher Vonheim. Though his name doesn't sound typically Norwegian, Ali is part of the Norwegian start-up scene and is just "typisk Norsk." He's a second-generation integrated Iraqi who appreciates what Norway offers. At the same time, he is an example of successful integration. Norway shows that the desire to achieve something and the willingness to work are the paths to successful integration and coexistence.

Ali's latest project is "Skyfri," meaning "Cloud-free." It's a modern platform for monitoring and controlling solar plants to maximize performance and reduce costs. His first company, Huddlestock, he founded in 2009, achieving stock market listings for both it and his second company, Norsk Solar, in 2020 and 2021, respectively—two within a year. He is a modern Viking making the world greener while building successful businesses, a serial entrepreneur of the new generation. Is Ali something like the Mark Zuckerberg of the blue and green economy? His visions extend, with "Skyfri," beyond the clouds and "Semypolky Solar" and "Gharo Solar," projects in Nicaragua, Pakistan, Ukraine, Vietnam, and Brazil. Ali travels the world, benefiting from the timing as Volodymyr Zelensky changed energy policy in Ukraine after his election in 2019 and found himself in a difficult situation with the outbreak of the COVID-19 pandemic and later the war. He has experienced all the highs and lows as a young entrepreneur.

In 2021, he announced his resignation to dedicate himself to his dissertation after an 8-year break, completing it under the title "Making the Impossible Possible." In it, Ali describes that it was only with his FinTech start-up Huddlestock that he managed to unite ecology and economy and what lessons he learned from the IPO of Norsk Solar with a valuation of almost 100 million euros.

Before the COVID-19 pandemic and the war in Ukraine, I was already searching for signs of a better future.

Looking back to 2018, the evening's atmosphere was electrifying at the Nordics CIO Executive Summit in Stockholm. After my brief dinner speech, I was approached by a board member of Statoil, the Norwegian oil giant. This board member represented a generation in Norway's boardrooms that tirelessly advocates diversity. She held the position not because of the quota; she had earned it and testifies to the success of the educational initiatives that have tried to make women's voices heard for decades.

Our conversation drifted toward the transformation of Statoil. The company, once synonymous with fossil fuels, was about to undergo a significant change. It was shedding its old identity and taking on the name Equinor—a name that evokes the idea of balance. Some might dismiss this as mere marketing, a facade. But the company not only aligns with the 2015 Paris Climate Agreement, but it also leads the way to a "Net Zero Future."

Four years later—in 2022—Equinor's shareholders and board have committed to an "energy transition plan" with the goal of halving emissions in all business areas, investing more than 50% in renewable energies and low-carbon markets, and reducing net carbon intensity by 20%, including emissions from the use of sold products—all by 2030. Their conviction is clear: "Science says we are moving too slowly, and we agree."

A year later, on August 8, 2023, Crown Prince Haakon of Norway inaugurated Hywind Tampen, the world's largest floating wind farm.

Who would have thought that this product would be "Made in Norway"?

Norwegian engineering is already a global export. Equinor's projects, ranging from the coasts of Norfolk to New York, supply millions of people and expand the boundaries of what's possible.

For me, this embodies the essence of progress. It's not about predicting the end, but about shaping a brighter, more sustainable future, indeed "better problems."

In the Norwegian autumn of 2018, six months after my first encounter with Equinor, I found myself again in Norway, at the leading start-up community Mesh Nationaltheatret in Oslo. The occasion was now the "Thinking Conference." My company for the evening? None other than Crown Prince Haakon of Norway and Aksel Lund Svindal, a name associated with alpine skiing. And here, today in retrospect, I met two representatives of the Viking Code. Both Crown Prince Haakon and Aksel Lund Svindal have embodied the typical Norwegian spirit of collective effort over the years and have committed to numerous social and ecological initiatives. They unwaveringly believe in progress and are committed to the collective. On this day, they joined a Norwegian "dugnad" of entrepreneurship.

At the forefront of this conference was Kjell Olav A. Maldum, a man whose passion for recycling has earned him the nickname "King of Recycling" from the Norwegian newspaper *Finansavisen*. Under Maldum's leadership, the Infinitum movement has redefined what it means to recycle in Norway.

And this is not a new trend; since 1902, Norway has had a deposit system for reusable bottles! It was a slow process, but the fruits of this labor have become apparent, as highlighted by the *Guardian* with the headline "Can Norway help us solve the plastic crisis, one bottle at a time?" Today, Norwegian companies are at the forefront of recycling, developing profitable models that serve as a guide worldwide. Names like Tomra, Metallco, Plastretur, and

Wastefront are in high demand, recycling everything from plastic and glass to aluminum and steel scrap.

And the world is taking notice.

In 2023, the United Kingdom, inspired by a century-old Norwegian tradition, introduced its own recycling program. This was a testament to the idea that progress sometimes does not mean reinventing the wheel but rather looking back, learning, and adapting. The country of Norway itself is a symbol of the Viking Code, benefiting from its early start and representing the pinnacle of the emerging Quantum Economy.

11

Infinite Progress

IN THE QUANTUM Economy, where the boundaries of the possible are constantly being redefined, humanity serves as our compass. It reminds us that in our pursuit of excellence, we must never lose sight of our vivacity—life itself. Ultimately, it's not about how advanced our technology is, but how we use it to enrich and inspire human experiences. The future may be uncertain, but with humanity as our guiding star, it can shine. We find shining examples of a new economy not just in Norway. If we look closer, there are many great initiatives; we just need more of them. Our efforts—our performance—must adhere to a set of values that enable the indefinite extension of organized human life on the planet.

With rapid optimization and constant growth, capitalism has given us a narrative of progress. However, this narrative has been shaped by a one-sided perspective dominated by short-term self-interests, a focus on profit maximization, and a wasteful disregard for the resources our planet has provided us. This approach is now being tested, as noticeable instability looms, constrained by finiteness. The true potential lies in progress, especially in technological advancement, driven by human effort and growth. Humans are at the center of this progress, possessing an enormous ability to develop better solutions and approaches. Both individually and collectively, we have the potential to drive positive development forward. In the past 50 years, we have seen a remarkable increase in the world's population from 3.5 to more than 8 billion people, driven by innovations and growth. This progress has so far followed a Newtonian approach to capitalism and economics, which is now undergoing a paradigm shift. In this new era, we must shift our focus from short-term self-interests and profit maximization to sustainable and responsible action.

A hundred years ago, one of the most significant shifts in scientific thinking occurred. Modern physics introduced us to complexity science and chaos theory. Paradigm shifts and revolutions in psychology, social science, and even capitalism as developed following Adam Smith were all products of Newtonian system thinking. Just as the "discovery" of quantum theory, new metaphors and perspectives for economics are now required. We are facing an upgrade of capitalism, where leaders and responsible creators learn to creatively deal with complexities and uncertainties. From Newtonian managers and players in an optimization- and hyper-efficiency society, creators of a new change are emerging. Leaders who learn (and love) to live with instability and uncertainty. They embrace complexities and understand that progress and destructive creations often exist "on the edge of chaos." Infinite players who toy with the limits of the game itself, aim to participate in the game as long as possible. It's not about abolishing structure and stability in management, but about a holistic understanding that often solves creative errors and risks "bottom-up" and self-organized, rather than "top-down" and hierarchical. We are—still—dealing with living organisms with brains and their own qualia—humans—who have their own needs and aspirations to understand their world. In interaction, a creative, dynamic force arises that will shape our future.

In such a new worldview, Newtonian organizations are no longer operated like machines but respected as living systems. From biology, we learn the approach to "complex adaptive systems." The emerging capitalism and the Quantum Economy, similar to other living systems, are in a constant, creative dance with their environment. They are sensitive, dynamic, and quickly adapt to changes. The global interdependencies and risks become part of the change, enabling the economy to free us from our old assumptions and detach us from our infected Newtonian thinking.

The Quantum Economy represents a transformative change in our worldview. At the heart of this new paradigm is humanity as an entity of hope, creativity, and potential. We strive from a fragmented knowledge society toward a holistic society of the mind, where uncertainty follows certainty. Our future consists of potentiality—what could be—allowing us to adaptively respond to future events.

In the next 10 years, the challenge will be to build a future where humanity does not place its hope solely on migrating to other planets. This will require an expansion of our way of thinking. The either/or paradigm is followed by a "both-and" approach. What "futures" can we anticipate?

By "anticipated future," I understand the mental anticipation or prediction of future events or states. This can happen on an individual level, within organizations, or in society as a whole. A key aspect here is anticipation, meaning the expectation or foreseeing of something that has not yet occurred. This includes planning and preparation for "the future." It's about scenarios and forecasts that understand the world as potentiality. This results in adaptability for future events. I refer here to any subjective expectations, hopes, and even fears about what our future might bring, as well as a sensitization for decisions in the present. We all can evidently influence—at least our own perceived—reality. If we have visions and expectations of the future, we can exert a strong influence on how people and organizations act in the present.

Engaging with the anticipated future is a way to deal with the inherent uncertainty of what lies ahead. By attempting to anticipate future developments, one can gain a sense of control or preparedness. Similar to athletes who mentally play through events in all possible scenarios to be prepared, this also leads to a desirable and worthwhile future worth striving for. This is of utmost importance at a time when increasingly rapid reactions are demanded instead of deep reflection as definitive answers. Walt Disney's saying, "If you can dream it, you can do it," has never been more relevant. Crucial here are the "ability" and the "action."

I view the anticipated future as an understanding for individual life management—my path—as well as for strategic planning that goes hand in hand with the successive goals of a Newtonian worldview. Progress is possible, infinite progress. It always moves forward.

If we look closely, we also find other perspectives and new insights that might offer a more purposeful path to a better future for humanity than the current reactionism. Simple changes in our viewpoint open up new possibilities.

What does our world really look like, and what can we anticipate from it? The debate around electromobility is complex: on one hand, it's said, "the transition to e-mobility is too slow," and on the other, some claim, "e-mobility is not the solution." In talk shows, the scarcity of rare earths and issues of "real" sustainability are discussed. These arguments sound plausible and are at least quotable, shareable, and likeable. However, upon closer examination, they seem more like a mix of theory and "doxa"—or "the chatter," as Heidegger called it—as opposed to practice and reality.

Elon Musk creates incentives for behavioral changes, and the industry responds to it. Even as hydrogen and new technology forms may gain importance, the world is currently building electric cars and their infrastructure. By 2035, the sale of combustion engines will be prohibited. This may not seem fast, but it's still a spark of hope for progress. By then, possibly new or better technologies could develop, promising even more progress. The reality of the transition, however, probably looks different, as electric cars will be cheaper than combustion engines over their entire lifecycle starting from 2025. New providers are emerging, and alongside Musk, Asian brands are penetrating the heart of the German automotive industry and economy: NIO with a production site in Berlin and a showroom in Munich, BAIC entering a joint venture with Mercedes and Hyundai, and SAIC, China's largest automaker, turn over hundreds of billions in revenue. Overnight, we see BYD (Build Your Dreams) on German roads—a company that already comes close to Tesla in sales numbers and sells more than twice as many electric vehicles as Volkswagen.

Sexy, innovative, and affordable—this is how the new mobility concepts from China present themselves. The German sleeping giant begins to stir. "Competition invigorates business," goes the old wisdom. How many similar narratives can we find here? The answer is: many.

What about the transition to green energy? A modern standard wind turbine can supply electricity to about 4,000 households. It is estimated that Germany would need about 40,000 wind turbines (including older generations and maintenance). That sounds like an incredibly high number, and with 8-year approval processes as well as lengthy and complex discussions, lack of risk-taking, and investment reluctance, one wonders how this is supposed to work. "The money is there," say the experts, but everything takes too long.

Surprisingly, however, it works. Germany has already built more than 30,000 onshore wind turbines! And that's just the wind from the land, not counting the potential of offshore wind and the incredible possibilities of photovoltaics or other energy forms for a green future. In a time of decadence and lack of commitment, what future is anticipated? What do we believe? What could we achieve if we managed to develop a new culture of performance?

What do you think? Will more global investments be made in the coming years? Will storage become more powerful, technologies more efficient, and production as well as commissioning cheaper? Will technology and business models be more profitable in the future?

Approximately 97,000 people traveled to the UN Climate Conference in Dubai, Cop 28, in 2023. Climate activists and media expressed criticism: wrong place and a doubling of travelers! To Cop 27 a year earlier, "only" 50,000 participants came. The headlines focused on private jets and environmental pollution, value understanding, and "greenwashing," and everything seemed bad. The major goal of phasing out fossil fuel use could not be adopted in 2023 either. But there's another perspective: twice as many people from new regions and countries, bringing even more money per person, travel to a region already undergoing rapid change. The United Arab Emirates and Saudi Arabia are far from perfect by European value standards, but a closer look reveals that development has taken place here in the last 10 years—the direction is right, even if it's not fast enough. Europe's development was also anything but linear, fast, and problem-free, so we must understand that breaking with old narratives and dogmas won't happen overnight and probably won't be smooth. But if it does happen, what does that mean for German and European competitiveness?

Even in the world of tomorrow, it will be about efficiency and cost-saving measures, but above all, about performance and progress. The future is happening now.

Perhaps a major COP in Dubai will turn more "black sheep" white, even if a bit of "washing" is required. As a cognitive irritation, 7.2 million people traveled to the last Oktoberfest. The

COP is far from perfect and not efficient, the world is not perfect, but where is the change happening? This question is relevant and of utmost importance, at least from a German and European perspective, and something the United States can adopt and follow.

For the big levers of change follow not only prohibitions, regulations, and reductions, but rather progress. I want to emphasize again that regulations are fundamentally important, as well as a change in behavior from a Western perspective—with Europe playing a central role. However, in my worldview, an anticipated future will look different. It's about competitiveness.

We often overestimate the short-term potential of technology and underestimate its medium- and long-term possibilities. This leads to the "sudden" emergence of new icons and market leaders, and we talk about a "technological revolution." In 10 to 15 years, when both the storage and distribution of solar and wind energy are expanded, what role will Europe play in global competition? Similar to car development, it will not be significant in which year fossil fuels are phased out, but rather from when they are no longer competitive. And from that follows the question: When they are no longer competitive, who determines the direction? This is a question very much relevant to the political course and the US economy.

Here too, we see that China, often portrayed as "the great villain" because of its coal power plants, owns the five largest photovoltaic companies in the world. In addition, China has a lower per capita energy consumption than most European countries and is rapidly catching up in the expansion of projects.

Just a few years ago, 80% of expansion projects in Europe were leading, but now we are being overtaken by the East and the South. We don't have energy problems per se, but mainly a storage and distribution problem. Don't you believe that humanity will also achieve technological progress here? Who will be the innovators and shapers of this new world?

As long as we believe and hold on to the fact that we are humans with our own creative potential, we are not calculable and predictable. Even though we operate in the visible realm—our perceived reality—and not in the very large or the subatomic small, the Heisenberg Uncertainty Principle is an apt metaphor for dealing with our system thinking involving humans. It states that the quantum mechanical properties of an object cannot be exactly determined simultaneously.

In the optimization society of the past decades, we have almost perfected the "art of being right" but have neglected the art of being wrong, or philosophy. The great implications of the uncertainty principle are that the questions we ask in each situation influence the answers we get—and the answers we don't get. We only see what we look for, or as Heisenberg put it: "We can focus on the position or the momentum of a particle, but never on both." This human shaping is subject to abilities that we find in the Viking Code: creativity, self-confidence, courage, dealing with deceptions, dreams, belief in progress. It's also about exploring something that might not make sense, or saying or doing something that is wrong for a long time, until it's right.

It is the human, vibrant, and social core of capitalism that ensures we do not stray from our path. The Quantum Economy, exploring the potential of technological progress, places humans at its center and emphasizes the symbiotic growth of man and technology. The Quantum Economy is not just a new—rigid—system, but rather a new understanding of society and economy. History is rich with examples where, at crucial turning points, the better judgment of humanity prevailed. Whether it was restraint during the Cold War, Gorbachev's decisions that steered us away from nuclear annihilation, or the collective decision not to pursue the alluring path of human cloning—time and again, we have shown that our moral compass, when heeded, guides us in the right direction. For this reason, I adhere to a positive and progress-oriented life philosophy.

This is exactly what characterizes the modern Vikings; this is the essence of the Viking Code.

Some threats, like nuclear warfare, are clear and immediate, casting a shadow that we can distinctly recognize. Others, however, like the gradual destruction of our environment, the multifaceted challenges of climate change, and the rapid rise of exponential technologies, present threats that are hard to quantify and often escape our immediate understanding. They are like puzzles within puzzles, requiring not only our attention but also profound introspection.

Indeed, with the immense power we possess comes an even greater responsibility. It's not just about tackling current challenges, but also ensuring that our actions today do not jeopardize the world of tomorrow. Our values, ethos, and commitment to the common good will determine the legacy we leave behind, and our decisions in creating digital superintelligence will significantly shape the continuation of human history.

In this era, we need an affirmative culture of togetherness, a collective effort, indeed a new performance culture deeply rooted in values. The human, with their infinite wisdom and compassion, must be our guiding star, ensuring that in our pursuit of progress, we do not lose sight of what truly matters.

Norway and its understanding of what it means to be successful can serve as a model for us in this regard.

First, it's about defining success.

If we restrict the definition of success to a Newtonian and materialistic one, we overlook the potential of the Viking Code. Understanding the dance between defined (absolute) goals and the path of progress, the interplay between mind and matter, man and his environment—the closeness to nature—we comprehend the potential of Norwegian philosophy. Rather than dwelling on "what is," the Viking Code represents a departure from materialism, revealing a new framework of thought where success and growth are considered holistically, adhering to a worldly dynamic. It is fascinating to realize that even the Norwegians themselves are not aware of this philosophy, but see their success as part of a liveliness.

And this is exactly what I understand as a new performance culture, deeply rooted in values. We humans are created to create. Without action—without performance—life is meaningless. Thus, through our actions, we give life meaning. A beautiful journey to nowhere with clear goals and direction. I like to describe this as "a new worldview"—a world understanding that is both anticipatory and creative. This also includes preparing for the unknown and concerns the individual—you and me—but also, as we have learned, organizations, systems, or society as a whole.

Our journey leads us from finite solutions to infinite possibilities, where both Planet Earth and humans are no longer just cogs in the economic machine. The Quantum Economy transcends traditional categorizations; it paints the vision of a future characterized by positive progress, boundless "better problems," and an ever-deepening understanding. At the center of this new economic paradigm is the mensch, embodying hope, potential, and active creation as the true source of growth and excellence.

Imagine the idea of compound interest. Not in the financial sense, but as a metaphor for the cumulative effect of constant efforts and investments. In Norway, the dividends of such interest are beginning to show. The blossoms of collective upliftment are unfolding, depicting the image of a nation that believes not only in progress but in infinite progress.

With a solid foundation in micro-ambitions and a deep understanding of the complex interplay of dependencies and complexities, Norway has begun on a course of progress. But this is not progress for its own sake. It's progress that understands the past, is grounded in the present, and vigilantly keeps an eye on the future.

The Viking Code is more than just a set of principles; it is a way of life that carries "dugnad" as the foundation of a strong culture. It promotes positivity and play, placing them at the center of creation. It's an enticing look into a future where Norway has emerged in recent decades as an inspiration for how to realize visions of renewable energy and meet the entire energy demand through technologies that are not just on the drawing board but already operational. If such an operating system for society succeeds, I look positively at our future.

To a technology utopia, I say, "Yes!"

The potential of technology is limitless.

Why do I believe this?

The simple answer is this: I find such a scenario realistic because it would prolong organized human life. I do not believe in a utopian effective accelerationism as promoted in the Techno-Optimist Manifesto of the likes of Marc Andressen, but more of a dynamic accelerationism that unleashes the potential of exponential technologies and human growth. I like to consider myself an advocate of scientific future optimism, but above all, it's about shifting our understanding of growth from mere optimization to human growth. With our unlimited access to knowledge and the increasingly powerful support of technology, it is up to us humans to shape a desirable future. Will it be easy? Of course not. But what are we theoretically capable of achieving collectively?

And this is exactly where the Viking Code comes into play.

We need performance, but this performance should benefit the collective. If the team becomes better, and I, as an individual, want to put in the effort, I can grow even more. It fundamentally relies on a shared understanding of values. If we can overcome negativity and reductionism, and focus on our minds, reasoning, behavior, and progress, immense possibilities await us. Experiencing progress and human growth is the true measure of success.

Epilogue: The Life in Itself

I DREAM OF a majestic tree. Its roots penetrate deep into the earth, drawing nourishment and strength. Its sturdy trunk supports branches that stretch out to embrace the sky. This tree is more than a symbol; it's a living representation of the magical triangle of our new definition of "growth." It embodies the dynamic equilibrium between our inner self and the external environment, between the values dear to us and the ever-changing world we navigate. Each branch, each leaf, tells a story of journeys undertaken and challenges overcome—a journey of life—of individual adventures contributing to a collective narrative.

In an age defined by rapid technological advancements, our true challenge lies not only in discovering what's achievable but in determining what's truly worth striving for, as the pace of progress is set to increase in the coming years.

What future is worth living?

Can you envision a world where we not only react based on data and technology but truly understand—where we grasp the depths and complexities of our surroundings—a world driven not just by knowledge, but by deep understanding and reason?

We evolve from reactive, profit-driven stakeholders to active creators of a future worth living.

Can we even imagine a future where "sustainability" has been transcended? Not because we neglect it, but because we master it and move beyond, or simply because it becomes an integral part of our economy and society? Or, to ask it differently: If we in fact could technologically build anything, what kind of world would we create?

This may sound far-fetched, but these are precisely the questions humanity will face over the next decade. To actively shape a desirable future, to move from reactive power to creative force, the Viking Code serves as a compass to design the operating system of our society.

Humans were not made for limitations. We are explorers, social beings, inherently programmed for discovery and connection. So when we talk about change, especially behavioral change, it should be about breaking existing boundaries and harnessing our innate urge to explore. The real catalyst for change is not fear or restriction; it's inspiration.

While grim predictions and doomsday scenarios may make headlines and boost sales, I've always chosen a path of hope and progress. Not necessarily because it's easier, but due to my unwavering optimism. After all, if the world were to end, who would be left to say, "I told you so"?

I admit, I have an ego and see myself reflected in the externalization and validation of goals, but above all, it's the intrinsic motivation to strive for "better problems" and progress and hope that drives me. The hope of learning and experiencing something new every day. I love the pursuit of truth, experiencing and recognizing the new—in the Beyond.

The Beyond—the "Jenseits"—I understand as a kind of metaphysical or spiritual dimension, fundamentally different from the real, everyday world—this side. It's the void, the unknown, that must be distinguished from the perceptible, the known. The Beyond represents a contrast between everyday reality and another, deeper state of being or consciousness.

Through our perception, through our feelings, we humans possess something special, but above all, we have the ability to fill our lives to achieve positive progress.

And that, for me, is true fulfillment.

This performance-oriented mindset, rooted in an ever-improving and stronger foundation of values, is my way of addressing all our current crises, not just the big global ones, but also the small, local, and subjective ones in our everyday lives.

And this, for me, is the quintessence of the Viking Code.

That we experience and recognize that achievement is beautiful, freeing us from the constant search for something—for a finite goal—and opening doors to new meaning, the pursuit of progress, access to infinity, and what makes us human: vibrancy. Life itself.

This side—the "Diesseits"—exhibits a brutal indifference. If it has a soul, it's cold. If it has perception, it's absent. It's ugly, brutal, and absurd. Yet, when we dive headfirst into the abyss, the light of vibrancy shines, and a new, beautiful absurdity can blossom. I call this the madness of the beyond—the "Jenseits."

Anders Indset
Røros, Norway
December 24, 2023

References

Preface

Hettl, M. (2018). Tall poppy syndrom. *Magazin Hettl Consult*. Available from: https://magazin.hettl-consult.de/tall-poppy-syndrom

Lützow, S. (2023). Sportwunder Norwegen: Warum ein kleines Land alles kann. *Der Standard*. Available from: https://www.derstandard.de/story/2000143788451/sportwunder-norwegen-warum-ein-kleines-land-alles-kann

Sandemose, A. (1999). En flyktning krysser sitt spor. Espen Arnakkes kommentarer til Janteloven, Oslo, S. 82.

Sima, J. (2023). Hur tusan blev Norge plötsligt bäst på allt. Aftonbladet. Available from: https://www.aftonbladet.se/ledare/a/RG0azd/sverige-vs-norge-en-storbrorsduell-om-titeln-som-bast-i-norden

Part 1

Ankersen, R. (2015). *The gold mine effect*. London: Icon Books

Dubner, S. J. and Levitt, S. (2005). *Freakonomics: A rogue economist explores the hidden side of everything*. New York City: William Morrow.

Chapter 1

Crouse, K. (2015, Nov. 20). Competitiveness seen as a virtue, at least for men. *New York Times*. Available from: https://www.nytimes.om/2015/11/20/sports/golf/suzann-pettersens-competitiveness-is-not-seen-as-the-virtue-it-is-for-men.html

McGuire, M. (2020). Suzann Pettersen: "I guess I would like to tell my story; the unfiltered story" [online]. LPGA Women's Network. Available from: https://lpgawomensnetwork.com/suzann-pettersen-i-guess-i-would-like-to-tell-my-story-the-unfiltered-story

Myklebust, K. (2023). Graham Hansen: – Janteloven står tydeligvis sterkt. Tipsbladet. https://tipsbladet.no/graham-hansen-janteloven-star-tydeligvis-sterkt

Chapter 2

Balyi, I., Weg, R., Higgs, C. (2013). Long-Term Athlete Development. Champaign: Human Kinetics.

Coyle, D. (2009). *A talent code: Greatness isn't born. It's grown. Here's how*. New York: Bantam.

Ericsson, A., Pool, R. (2016). *Peak: Secrets from the New Science of Expertise*. New York: Houghton Mifflin Harcourt.

Gladwell, M (2008). *Outliers: The Story of Success*. New York: Little, Brown and Company.

Stenvold, I. (2021). *A winner's heart: The Marit Bjørgen story*. Oslo: Kagge Forlag.

Chapter 3

Bräuer, Sebastian (2023): Die erfolgreichste Männer-WG der Welt: Drei Norweger provozieren die Triathlonszene, Neue Zürcher Zeitung. https://www.nzz.ch/sport/die-erfolgreichste-maenner-wg-der-welt-drei-norweger-provozieren-die-triathlonszene-ld.1729538?reduced=true

Collins, J. (2012). Oben bleiben. Immer, Frankfurt am Main,

Pink, D. H. (2020). *Drive:* Was Sie wirklich motiviert, Elsbethen,

Chapter 4

Cars, J.P. (2013). *Finite and infinite games.* New York: Free Press.

Clear, J. (2020). Die 1%-Methode – Minimale Veränderung, maximale Wirkung: Mit kleinen Gewohnheiten jedes Ziel erreichen - Mit Micro Habits zum Erfolg, Frankfurt am Main,

Covey, S. R. (1989). *The 7 habits of highly effective people.* New York City: Simon & Schuster.

Hardy, D. (2012). *The Compound Effect: Jumpstart Your Income, Your Life, Your Success.* Vanguard Press.

Hoppmann, E. H. (2019). Wie ein norwegischer Vater seine Söhne zu Weltklasseläufern machte, Spiegel Sport. https://www.spiegel .de/sport/sonst/leichtathletik-wm-die-erfolgsstory-der-familie-ingebrigtsen-a-1289334.html

Seligman, M. E. P. (1975). *Helplessness: On Depression, Development, and Death.* San Francisco: W.H. Freeman.

Chapter 5

Brown, S. (2010). *Play: How it shapes the brain, opens the imagination, and invigorates the soul.* New York City: Avery.

Carse, J. P. (2013). *Finite and infinite games.* New York: Free Press

Dean, S. (2023). Martin Odegaard: 'What happened last season made Arsenal angry.' *Telegraph* [online]. Available from: https:// www.telegraph.co.uk/football/2023/02/10/martin-odegaard-people-think-nice-guy-have-fire-inside

Fredheim, G. O. (2019). Warholm: - Barn må ikke spesialisere seg tidlig for å bli best, Norges Idrettsforbund. https://www.idrettsforbundet .no/nyheter/2019/barn-ma-ikke-spesialisere-seg-tidlig-for-a-bli-best

Norris, R. (2023). Here's how to get the maximum mood boost from your workout, according to sports psychologists. *well+good* [online]. Available from: https://www.wellandgood.com/mood-boosting-workout

Chapter 6

Putnam, R. (2020). *The upswing: How America came together a century ago and how we can do it again.* New York City: Simon & Schuster.

Chapter 8

Arendt, H. (1960). Vita activa oder Vom tätigen Leben, Stuttgart.

Bovell, S. (n.d.). About Sinead Bovell [online]. Available from: https://sineadbovell.com/aboutsinead

Englisch Ausgabe von Trudy Dixon (Herausgeber), Shunryu Suzuki (Autor), Platon: Apologie 22d, Übersetzung von Friedrich Schleiermacher, bearb. von Heinz Hofmann, 5. Aufl., WBG, Darmstadt 2005, S. 17.

Kant, I. (1784). Beantwortung der Frage: Was ist Aufklärung? Berlinische Monatsschrift«, DezemberHeft S. 48–494.

Nietzsche, F. (1873). *Unzeitgemäße Betrachtungen [Untimely meditations].* Leipzig.

Norwegens Staatsfonds im Plus, Sueddeutsche Zeitung. https://www .sueddeutsche.de/wirtschaft/norwegen-staatsfonds-1.6133899# :~:text=Das%20Volumen%20des%20Fonds%20stieg,sowie% 20%C3%9Cberweisungen%20der%20norwegischen%20 Regierung

Nussbaum, M. C. (2000). *Women and human development: The capabilities approach.* Cambridge: Cambridge University Press.

Rawls, J. (1971). *A theory of justice.* Cambridge, MA: Harvard University Press.

Rorty, R. (2002). *Education, philosophy, and politics (Critical media studies: Institutions, politics, and culture).* Lanham: Rowman & Littlefield.

Sullivan, J. (2019). *With second world title, Warholm joins all-time 400m hurdles greats* [online]. World Atheltics. Available from: https://worldathletics.org/news/feature/karsten-warholm-400m-hurdles-doha-champion

Suzuki, S. (2011). *Zen mind, beginner's mind (rohschnitt auflage): Informal talks on zen meditation and practice.* Shambhala.

Chapter 9

Calomiris, C. W. and Haber, S. H. (2014). *Fragile by design: The political origins of banking crises and scarce credit*. Princeton: Princeton University Press.

Derrida, J. (2002). *Politik der Freundschaft*, Übersetzt von Lorenzer, Stefan, Berlin.

Deutsch, D. (2011). *The beginning of infinity: Explanations that transform the world*. New York: Penguin.

Greene, R. (1998). *The 48 laws of power*. New York City: Penguin Books.

Hirschmann, A. O. (1970). *Exit, voice and loyalty: Responses to decline in firms, organizations and states*. Cambridge, MA: Harvard University Press.

Luhmann, Niklas; Maturana, Humberto R.; Varela, Francisco J.: Der Baum der Erkenntnis. Die biologischen Wurzeln des Erkennens, München 1987.

MBO Partners. (2023). *Digital nomads*. Available from: https://www.mbopartners.com/state-of-independence/digital-nomads

Orwell, G. (1949). *1984*. London: Secker & Warburg.

Postman, N. (1995). *Amusing ourselves to death: Public discourse in the age of show business*. New York City: Penguin.

Srinivasan, B. (2022). *The network state: How to start a new country*. Amazon Kindle.

Steuer, H. (2023). Ukraine treibt die digitale Verwaltung auch im Krieg voran. Handelsblatt, https://www.handelsblatt.com/politik/international/govtech-ukraine-treibt-die-digitale-verwaltung-auch-im-krieg-voran/29410418.html

Taleb, N. N. (2013). *Antifragilität: Anleitung für eine Welt, die wir nicht verstehen*. München.

Chapter 10

Sinek, S. (2019). Das unendliche Spiel: Strategien für dauerhaften Erfolg, München,

About the Author

Anders Indset—KNOWN AS the business philosopher—is a Norwegian-born writer, investor, and former elite athlete. He is a four-time Spiegel best-selling author, author of six international books, and has been recognized by Thinkers50 as one of the influential thinkers in the fields of technology and leadership in the years to come. He is a trusted sparring partner and advisor for global leaders and top executives and the founder of Njordis Group, Global Institute of Leadership & Technology (GILT), and the Quantum Economy Alliance.

Index

227